LEADING BY DESIGN

The Insider's Playbook
For Tech Leadership

SALLY GRISEDALE

sg

Author photography by Rhee Bevere, www.rheebeverephoto.com.

Leading by Design /Grisedale, Sally. -- 1st ed.

Published by Prominence Publishing, www.prominencepublishing.com.

ISBN Paperback: 978-1-997649-16-8
ISBN Hardcover: 978-1-997649-06-9

Table of Contents

*"Almost always, the creative,
dedicated minority has made the world better."*
Martin Luther King, Jr.

Introduction

In March of 1997, I was invited by the International Institute for Information Design to be a guest speaker at the *Vision Plus 4: The Republic of Information* symposium at the School of Design at Carnegie Mellon University in Pittsburgh. They had heard of my work with midwives in rural India for Apple and wanted me to give a presentation on what we had been doing there. It was an incredible honor and an experience I will never forget. I left feeling proud of our work and the presentation I had given, but didn't think anything else would come from the weekend. Well, it turns out I was wrong.

Eight years later, I found myself in Beijing, China, co-sponsoring an executive forum called *The Design for the New China Markets Conference*. After the conference presentations, I took a group of my Yahoo colleagues and friends to dinner at the Red Capital Club restaurant. During dinner, one person in our group mentioned that they had seen me give a presentation about my work in India at Carnegie Mellon University. They explained that witnessing how we initiated our research and user-centered design process to develop mobile software for rural healthcare nurses inspired them to pursue a career in user experience design (UXD).

Those intervening eight years had been a whirlwind for me. I transitioned from being deep in the future at Apple's Advanced Technology Group, exploring cutting-edge user interaction, to suddenly facing a total reset due to the lab's closure after Steve Jobs' return, a visa cliffhanger, and my father's passing.

Bouncing back, I navigated the design agency world briefly before landing at Excite!, shaping web experiences for millions and getting a glimpse of the mobile future. Then came the rocket ship that was Yahoo, where I joined as their first design manager and built a team that supercharged their media services. We're talking about tangible impact—boosting user numbers, climbing market ranks, and driving serious revenue.

That momentum propelled me to become a director, leading teams and establishing a strong design culture and strategic integration. It was a period of intense growth, unexpected challenges, and significant personal and professional development. From individual contributor to senior director, I navigated layoffs, visa battles, and the ever-evolving tech landscape.

Growing up in rural Berkshire, England, in the 80s, the idea of leading user experience design teams in tech was utterly foreign. So, when Apple called on the eve of my Royal College of Art graduation, inviting me to their Human Interface Group at 1 Infinite Loop, in Cupertino, California, I nearly said no. Leave Andy, my fiancé, for California? Ludicrous! Yet, destiny intervened. I found myself at Heathrow, waving goodbye and embarking on a 29-year odyssey through Apple, Yahoo, Meta, a design agency, and an AI startup, ultimately building my executive coaching practice for design leaders.

Sitting at the Red Capital Club restaurant after those eight long, challenging, beautiful years, something shifted in me. Hearing that my story had impacted someone's career so deeply meant a lot to me, and it helped me see how much more I could be doing.

That's why I'm writing *Leading by Design*. This book is my way of guiding the next generation of creative leaders—those who, like me, stumbled into leadership, driven by the belief that good design is good business. After nearly three decades of navigating the intricacies of interaction design, management, and executive leadership, I've witnessed firsthand what it takes to ascend to the C-suite and flourish. I aim to equip you with the confidence, influence, and preparedness to tackle the challenges ahead.

While ample guidance exists for individual and design manager roles, the path to executive design leadership remains largely uncharted. This book is my attempt to fill that void. It's a practical, experience-driven guide enriched by insights from seven exceptional executive thought leaders in engineering, product management, and user experience design who generously shared their journeys into the tech world and their ascent to executive leadership. They are Robert Girling, co-founder of the award-winning design agency Artifact; Colin Grigson, the design director at Remitly; Lynn Bacigalupo, the product manager at Icomera; Julie Baher, vice president of customer experience and digital strategy at Myriad Genetics; Phil Clevenger, vice president of product experience at DocuSign; Ajay Thakur, head of cognitive computing at Uber; and Anshuman Kumar, the senior vice president and head of design at Asana.

We'll delve into the history of design in tech, how businesses perceive our role, and the metrics that matter to C-suite executives. You'll learn to strategically position yourself within your organization and build strong relationships with cross-functional partners. Crucially, we'll explore the significance of self-leadership and nurturing healthy relationships in your new role. I'll share practical strategies for building alliances, neutralizing saboteurs, inspiring fence-sitters, and channeling the energy of provocateurs.

Now, more than ever, the world needs creative designers to shape the future with thoughtfully designed, tested, and deployed products and services. Join me on this transformative journey, and let's craft a powerful design narrative that speaks the language of humanity and data and firmly establishes your place at the executive table.

CHAPTER 1

How to Get the Top Job

CHARTING YOUR COURSE TO THE TOP

This chapter explores opportunities to help you position yourself for a top design leadership role at a tech company, regardless of its size or growth stage. It serves as your strategic roadmap, illuminating the path to executive leadership and equipping you with the insights needed to land the role and thrive. We'll begin by charting the typical career trajectories leading to the executive suite, emphasizing the crucial stages of deep design mastery, early leadership cultivation, and the progressive expansion of strategic influence.

For those ready to leap, we will explore practical strategies for positioning yourself and navigating the transition from senior management to executive leadership. Preparation is key, and we'll guide you through the essential steps of understanding and articulating your strengths, values, and leadership capabilities—even translating them into the monetary language of the tech industry. We'll then demystify the executive hiring process, providing you with the tools to excel in your interviews and negotiate your offer with the savvy of your future business peers. Next, we'll delve into the real-world expectations placed upon those at the helm of design for a tech company or its division, providing a clear picture of what success truly looks like.

Finally, to bring this journey to life, we will hear firsthand from Phil Clevenger, VP and Head of Design at DocuSign, who will share his invaluable experiences and insights on advancing your design leadership career and securing the top job.

FOUNDATIONAL EXCELLENCE AND EARLY LEADERSHIP

Develop Deep Domain Expertise

The first five years of your career working in tech are your time to become highly proficient in one or more core design disciplines relevant to tech (e.g., product design, user experience design, user interface design, branding design, visual design, interaction design, service design, design operations, etc.). You continuously hone your craft and stay updated with the latest tools and trends. You build a strong portfolio of projects that showcase your problem-solving process, design decisions, range, and ability to tackle complex challenges, as well as the impact of your designs.

Along the way, you gain a solid understanding of the technology you're designing for, including its limitations, capabilities, and business implications.

Now, before we continue, if you are not a designer but an aspiring executive leader, please substitute design with your own area of domain expertise. Almost all of the advice given here will still apply to you.

Gain Early Management Experience

Seek opportunities to lead small teams or projects, guide junior team members, mentor others, or take ownership of significant project components. This could involve leading design sprints, managing feedback processes, or defining design direction for smaller initiatives. I was dismayed when my manager at Apple asked me to lead an interdisciplinary team that would research and design new information display prototypes. The three people I managed had vastly different skills, compensation, and domain expertise from my own. One was a highly respected Mac Operating Engineer (OS), a genius mechanical engineer, a brilliant interaction designer, and a fellow Royal College of Art alumnus. My very first staff meeting completely redefined my understanding of what a manager does. We kicked off by sharing individual responsibilities, unique work products, and preferred collaboration processes. From this foundation, we collaboratively developed a "North Star" vision and then worked backward to make it a reality. This group's inherent self-motivation was a pleasant surprise, quite unlike my expectations of management, and I genuinely enjoyed every minute.

Taking on the role of manager also meant stepping up to present our team's and the lab's work at Apple developer conferences. This required me to quickly enhance my presentation skills. Luckily, this challenge was made easier by the abundance of world-class role models within the lab, all ready to offer advice, and the exceptional quality of their work featured in the demo reel I was presenting.

What was harder for me to learn and appreciate was using my active listening skills (versus feeling the need to have an answer), giving constructive feedback (separating my feelings from facts), and collaborating with colleagues who may or may not care about or understand design. These skills, together with project management knowledge of timelines, resource allocation, and stakeholder management, are all prerequisites for executive leadership.

EXPAND YOUR FOCUS AND INFLUENCE

Lead Larger and More Complex Initiatives

After your fifth and before your tenth year in tech, your goal should be to take direct management of cross-functional teams, including hiring, mentoring, giving performance reviews, and fostering a positive and productive design culture. Go beyond design execution and contribute to product strategy to understand how design can drive business goals and user value. Learn to work effectively with engineering, product management, marketing, and other departments. Navigate different perspectives and build consensus. Developing cross-functional collaboration skills will make you the go-to person for design thought leadership. If a promotion is warranted, your allies across various functions will become essential partners in your advancement to executive management.

Connect Projects to the Bottom Line

My role as Yahoo's inaugural Design Manager in 2001 was a true eye-opener, revealing the immense strategic potential of **customer-inspired, data-driven design**. I led the user experience design for a wide array of websites, such as News, Finance, Movies, Kids, Games, Health, Sports, and Weather. Over two years, I successfully built and scaled a cross-functional media group design team of about 35 full-time staff, including experts in visual design, interaction design, design management, web development, and user research.

"Good design is good business."
Tom Watson Jr. and Elliott Noys, 1966, IBM

Build Your Professional Network

Throughout my career, I've learned that building a strong professional network isn't merely about collecting contacts; it's about fostering meaningful connections that can significantly influence your growth as a leader. Actively participating in industry events and conferences has consistently been invaluable in my career journey, offering opportunities not just to stay updated on emerging trends and innovative approaches but also to build relationships with other design leaders facing similar challenges and opportunities. Engaging with the wider design community—whether by contributing to online forums, sharing insights on design blogs, or mentoring—further enhances your presence and promotes a sense of reciprocal learning and support. Perhaps most impactful for me has been seeking mentorship from leadership coaches. Their guidance and hard-earned wisdom have provided crucial perspectives and support as I've navigated the complexities of leadership. Remember, your network is a vital ecosystem for learning, growth, hiring, and unlocking future opportunities. A good daily habit is to ask yourself, "Who do I need to lead or connect with today, and how can I do it well?"

HOW TO POSITION YOURSELF FOR THE TOP JOB

Refer Others and Get Referred

According to Jobvite, referrals account for 30-50% of new hires and likely an even higher percentage for executive positions. Often, the loose connections we keep with industry insiders— those distant acquaintances without any reporting lines or power dynamics—can lead you to your next opportunity. Loose ties wane if there isn't some reciprocity; therefore, be generous in referring those who have supported or assisted you in their careers, as they might be the connections to your next role.[1] A loose tie put me on the path to becoming a Chief Design Officer. I was at a Yahoo alumni gathering, catching up with a former colleague who asked me what I wanted to do next. Without hesitation, I said I wanted to build a user-experience design team from the ground up. Serendipitously, he knew of such an opportunity and connected me with Sequoia Venture Capital, which was actively seeking the right leader to establish a design team for one of their portfolio companies. Within a month, I was hired to create a global design studio as a core source of competitive advantage for the company.

---

[1] Karen Wickre. Taking the Work Out of Networking: Your Guide to Making and Keeping Great Connections. 2019.

Move From a Mature Company to a Startup

Another path to a top job is moving from a mature company to a startup. Suppose you've learned to lead projects and teams at a mature tech company, but the opportunity to further expand your leadership skills is limited by the sheer volume of top talent surrounding you. In that case, it may be time to transition to a startup to continue developing your leadership skills and ultimately attain a top position. Anshuman Kumar began his career as an individual contributor leading interaction design at Yahoo in the e-commerce business unit. His career progressed to project leadership roles and design management at Google, where he spent nine years pioneering the design of smartphones and augmented reality products. By moving from a mature company to the growth phase at Asana, he enhanced his executive leadership capabilities as Head of Design in one division. Within three years, he rose to Senior Vice President and Head of Design for the entire organization. You can read about his journey to the top job in Chapter Five.

Start Your Own Company

There's a saying that everyone in tech has a startup within them, inspiring them to launch their own company. Robert Girling exemplified this when he co-founded the award-winning strategy and design firm Artefact in Seattle. After a successful career at Apple, Microsoft, and IDEO, Rob teamed up with Gavin Kelly, a former Microsoft colleague, to help business leaders harness the power of design to create meaningful change and make a positive impact. You can read about Rob's journey from designing for big tech to executive entrepreneur in Chapter Three.

Carving Out Your Specialist Niche

Suppose you excel in deep design work and strategic collaboration with founders and technical teams. In that case, pursuing a specialist niche within early-stage tech companies can be a highly valued and lucrative path. These companies often seek contract-to-hire experts to infuse innovation and drive progress during their initial phases. As a founding designer, early-stage designer, mentor, or advisor, you play a crucial role in developing scalable concepts or minimum viable products (MVPs) that can be used to secure essential funding. These roles provide a unique opportunity to directly shape a growing company's foundational design language and user experience. Typically, specialists stay until the company reaches a scaling turning point and the focus shifts to broader team management. At this point, they often transition to another early-stage venture, bringing their expertise to new challenges. Specialized recruitment firms cater to this demand, connecting talented individuals with exciting startup opportunities on platforms like StartupHire, VentureFizz, and VentureLoop. If your passion lies in partnering closely with founders on design strategy and execution, without intending to manage design organizations, this specialist track offers a highly sought-after and rewarding career trajectory.

Get Promoted Internally

Internal promotion is one of the most straightforward paths to a top role. I joined a privately held startup as the first VP of Design, reporting directly to the Chief Technology Officer (CTO). More than a year later, at a women's leadership dinner, the CEO pulled me aside and asked if I would take on the role of Chief Design

Officer. It was an unexpected and delightful surprise, and I was excited to accept it.

After dinner, our Chief Financial Officer, who organized the event, encouraged everyone to share something about themselves and their career aspirations. When it was my turn, I announced that I had been invited to become the Chief Design Officer earlier that evening. The women raised their glasses to me and asked how I felt. I told them I felt flattered, excited, and like an impostor, but I'd work hard to turn that around, and I did.

Stepping into executive leadership is a fundamental shift in how you think, allocate your time, and engage with people. Before diving into the practicalities of preparing for an executive role, it's incredibly valuable to connect with your intrinsic leadership drivers, understand your inherent leadership strengths, and clearly articulate how your past work already showcases these strengths as a tangible value proposition.

Now that we've looked at how you can position yourself well to get the top job, our next section will focus on defining who you are as a leader—your essence—rather than merely outlining what you will do in the role. This is about strategically refining and amplifying your personal and professional brand. Who are you as an executive leader?

We'll work on crystallizing your brand narrative by crafting compelling stories that vividly illustrate the depth of your technical impact and the strength of your leadership. These stories will be invaluable assets when you engage with executive board members, deliver presentations and interviews, and refine your resume, social media presence, and LinkedIn profile. The goal is cultivating a reputation that precedes you, creating a situation where your accomplishments and leadership speak for themselves, and fostering an environment where others naturally advocate for your capabilities.

SELF-REFLECTION: UNDERSTAND YOUR LEADERSHIP STRENGTHS

Self-reflection is a process of clarifying the deep-seated emotions that fuel your desire to guide and inspire others. Uncovering your core motivations brings you a profound sense of clarity and confidence, instilling trust in those who will look to you for direction. Perhaps even more importantly, this self-awareness cultivates the resilience you'll need to weather the inevitable storms of leadership.

"To me, a leader is someone who holds her or himself accountable for finding potential in people and processes."
Brené Brown

The path to understanding your leadership 'why' is rarely linear or prescribed. For some, the call to lead may have been a lifelong knowing, while for others, it might have emerged unexpectedly from a passion for creation and building. You might have found yourself stepping into leadership through a stretch opportunity, surprised to discover a deep satisfaction in shaping organizations as much as shaping products—a realization I experienced, finding immense joy in building inclusive design cultures and empowering talent globally.

When I reflect on the opportunities I've been given and the privilege I've had to pay it forward, I'm reminded of the importance of timing and preparation. Part of that preparation involves introspective work to clarify your values and strengths. Tools like the Gallup StrengthsFinder helped me identify a core attribute: being a catalyst for new ways of thinking.[2] This resonates deeply as I recognize that I feel most aligned with my purpose as a leader when I'm in that catalytic role.

Know What Motivates You As a Leader

Another assessment I found helpful in understanding my motivation for leadership was reading about the type of person you are. Are you the Social Person, a natural connector and communicator who excels at building relationships but may need to develop a deeper understanding of systems and details? Or do you identify as the Ideas Person, a visionary brimming with innovation and new concepts, though sometimes challenged by follow-through? Do you see yourself as the Systems Person, an introverted yet highly detail-oriented individual who excels at optimizing processes and providing support, even though social interaction may not come naturally? Or are you the Supportive Energy Person, adept at helping others achieve their visions to empower themselves, someone skilled at enabling others to reach their full potential? This is my natural genius, my intrinsic motivation and purpose in life. Take a moment to reflect: Which of these descriptions resonates with you the most?

Understand Your Leadership Strengths

While a variety of executive leadership assessment tools exist, each offering unique insights—from the personality-focused Myers-Briggs Type Indicator (MBTI) and DISC to the

---

[2] From Gallup, Tom Rath. StrengthsBased Leadership: Great Leaders, Teams, and Why People Follow. From Gallup, 2008.

emotionally intelligent lenses of EQ-i 2.0 and MSCEIT, and the comprehensive 360-degree feedback of The Leadership Circle Profile (LCP) and the personality-driven Hogan Assessments— the 'best' choice truly hinges on the specific objectives, the organizational environment, and your leadership level. To empower leaders, I utilize the Gallup Leadership Strengths assessment. This tool helps them not only pinpoint their unique commercial value but also effectively communicate and illustrate it through impactful storytelling.

- **Executing**: How to make things happen

- **Influencing**: Empowering organizations to reach a much broader audience

- **Relationship building**: Building organizations greater than the sum of their parts

- **Strategic thinking**: Creating organizations aligned with what could be

Within each leadership domain are different themes. For instance, if one of your strengths lies in relationship building and you lead with the theme of Connectedness, this signifies a deep-seated belief in the interconnectedness of all things. This is your ability to effortlessly build trust, extend compassion, provide a sense of stability, and inspire hope within your teams. Conversely, if your relationship-building prowess leans toward the theme of Empathy, your ability to intuitively understand and share the feelings of others and step into their experience will help you deeply understand others' perspectives; an invaluable trait, especially in a user research context.

Connect Your Domain Strengths to Your Achievements

The practical application of leadership assessment reports lies in connecting the insights to your most recognized and results-driven work. A highly effective way to construct your success narrative is to use the SOAR (Situation, Obstacle, Action, Result) technique.[3]

SOAR offers a clear and logical structure making it easy for people to follow your narrative and grasp your contributions. Here's an example of someone who excels at building relationships, using the SOAR method to convey their strength through a value proposition at an interview.

"During a major company rebranding *(situation),* isolated teams with differing priorities and communication styles created tension and hindered progress *(obstacle.)* By building relationships through cross-functional workshops, open communication, and team-building activities *(action),* I cultivated a collaborative environment that led to a successful, timely, and budget-friendly rebranding launch with a consistent brand experience across all touchpoints *(result)."* Here is the same story told using the SOAR structure in a single sentence on their resume. "Unified siloed teams through targeted workshops, ensuring a 100% on-time and on-budget rebranding with consistent messaging."

Articulating your experiences through the lens of your inherent strengths allows you to craft uniquely powerful success stories—stories that only you can authentically tell. When you frame your career achievements around your natural abilities,

---

[3] Stavros, J. M., Cooperrider, D. L., & Kelley, D. L. (2003). Strategic inquiry appreciative intent: Inspiration to SOAR, a new framework for strategic planning. AI Practitioner, 11(3), 1-21.

rather than relying solely on company successes or brand recognition, you present an undeniable value proposition rooted in your intrinsic gifts. This makes your accomplishments irrefutable, as they stem from the core of who you are as a leader. Once polished and refined, your SOAR stories can be used on repeat in short or long form to help people understand what you stand for, what you can achieve, and how you can help them.

Having gained a deeper understanding of your core leadership identity and the unique value you bring as an executive—essentially, who you are as a leader—we will now focus on the practical aspects of navigating the executive hiring landscape in the tech industry. The insights you've gathered about your strengths and how to articulate your impact will serve as a solid foundation as we explore the process of preparing for and excelling in executive design interviews.

ABOUT THE EXECUTIVE TECH HIRING PROCESS

Would you like a clear pathway to pursuing the top job? It may not be as straightforward as lower-level positions where job levels and descriptions are easily found online or within your current organization. Executive positions are often defined more by the organization's needs and an individual's leadership qualities than by a specific list of responsibilities.

What? No Job Description?

It's uncommon to find clearly defined job descriptions for top-level roles, and there are several reasons for this. Senior leadership positions are, by their nature, very broad, requiring extensive strategic oversight and the ability to make critical decisions.

Attempting to define and measure these complex attributes within a standardized job description can be incredibly difficult. Furthermore, an overly strict job description might restrict the flexibility essential for these roles and discourage highly qualified candidates from applying. Finally, publicly disclosing a detailed job description could compromise confidentiality, disrupt internal operations, or create a perception of instability among stakeholders. This instability might be triggered by factors such as a current occupant being promoted or let go, broader organizational changes, or a re-evaluation of the role's scope.

The Role Executive Recruiters Play

Tech companies often collaborate with executive search firms to find and recruit top talent. You can build relationships with executive search firms and in-house executive recruiters by connecting on LinkedIn, scheduling introductory calls to discuss your career goals and experiences, and sharing your resume and portfolio with them. If you are brought in for an interview at big tech, you will work with a dedicated recruiter from start to onboarding. They will provide valuable information about the company, the hiring process, benefits, company values and mission, etc. They are typically incentivized to close executive hires, so they will be invaluable to you and want to see you succeed. They can be your sounding board through the often lengthy process that can take several months to complete, depending on many factors, including which quarter the budget is released to pay your salary. Be aware that they are also gathering feedback about you from interviewers during the interview process and will let you know where you stand in real time. It can be daunting to hear that "So and so didn't think you answered the xyz question to their satisfaction," but you'll also hear things like "Your group presentation was well-received," and "You are being considered for another role in a different team. Could you stay over another night to meet with that group?" Feedback isn't always fun, but it's always valuable, so make sure to use it!

EXPECTATIONS FOR THE TOP JOB

You're on the cusp of defining the next chapter of your career. Here's a quick summary of the broad scope your new role in the top job will encompass.

Defining and Driving Design Vision and Strategy

You'll architect the future direction of design, setting aspirational standards and crafting a comprehensive strategy that directly fuels business objectives and deeply resonates with user needs. This involves continuously under-standing market trends, anticipating user evolutions, and translating those insights into a compelling and actionable design roadmap.

Quantifying Your Team's Business Impact [4]

You are a champion for design's tangible value. You will rigorously measure and articulate design initiatives' return on investment (ROI). By strategically leveraging data analytics, user research findings, and a deep understanding of business metrics, you will demonstrate unequivocally that design is not a cost center but a fundamental driver of business success, influencing key outcomes like revenue growth, customer acquisition, and brand loyalty.

---

[4] "Defining the role of a chief design officer." *McKinsey*. Accessed May 5, 2025. https://www.mckinsey.com/capabilities/mckinsey-digital/our-insights/business-value-of-design/interactives/defining-the-role-of-a-chief-design-officer

Communicating with Influence

Your communication transcends design jargon. You will master the art of conveying design concepts and their strategic importance to diverse audiences, including the company's senior leadership team, industry peers, customers, and internal stakeholders. Using clear, concise, and business-focused language, you will present design narratives that align with overarching business goals, fostering understanding and buy-in at all levels.

Building and Scaling World-Class Design Organizations

As a leader, you are a magnet for attracting creative talent. You will strategically plan, budget, and build high-performing, cross-functional design organizations on domestic and, most likely, international scales. This involves a dedicated focus on attracting, nurturing, and empowering creative teams and their leaders across a broad spectrum of design disciplines, from foundational visual and interaction design to cutting-edge areas like AI and sustainable design. Your ultimate objective is to cultivate a collaborative and innovative environment where diverse perspectives converge to deliver exceptional user experiences.

Championing User-Centricity

You'll champion user needs, making sure their insights are not only heard, but truly drive product development and all key decisions. Your leadership will embed a user-first mindset throughout the organization, fostering a culture where empathy and a deep understanding of the user become central to how the business operates.

Cultivating a Culture of Innovation

You are the catalyst for creative breakthroughs. You will actively cultivate a vibrant culture of innovation, experimentation, and intellectual curiosity within your design teams. By fostering an environment where pushing boundaries, exploring unconventional solutions, and embracing calculated risks are encouraged, you will empower your teams to create groundbreaking and impactful designs.

Driving Performance and Accountability

You are a strategic leader focused on results. You will translate overarching business goals into clear and measurable KPIs for your design teams. You will then hold your teams accountable for achieving these KPIs through monitoring, constructive feedback, and performance reviews, ensuring that design efforts directly contribute to the company's corporate, business, and function goals.

Investing in Team Growth and Organizational Sustainability

You will be deeply invested in the continuous hiring, development, and mentorship of your team members, fostering their professional growth and ensuring your design organization's long-term health and sustainability. Crucially, you will also actively cultivate future leaders within your team and plan for your succession, providing a resilient, sustainable, thriving design function.

Collaborating for Holistic Product Excellence

You are a key orchestrator of the product vision. You will forge strong, collaborative partnerships with your counterparts in product management, engineering, and marketing. By fostering open communication and mutual understanding, you will ensure a cohesive, user-focused approach that profoundly influences the product roadmap and results in a unified user experience across all customer touchpoints.

Staying at the Forefront of Innovation and Market Dynamics

You'll be instrumental in proactively tracking technological advancements and analyzing competitor product strategies and differentiators, feeding these insights directly into your team and development process. This will be key to informing and shaping your design strategy, guaranteeing your team consistently delivers innovative and competitive solutions.

With a clear grasp of these expectations, your next step is to powerfully articulate why you are the ideal candidate for this role.

ELEVATE YOUR INTERVIEW GAME

The interview for an executive role demands a distinct level of precision and preparation. It's about anticipating the nuanced questions, demonstrating foresight, and showcasing your unique executive presence. You will likely know this already, so consider this section your essential checklist, designed to help you meticulously prepare, refine your narrative, and confidently demonstrate that you are the visionary leader their team needs.

Test the Product Experience

Before your interview, take the time to learn about the products and services by testing out the customer experience. This will tell you a lot about the company's investment in user-experience design and ensure you are well-informed to ask relevant questions and provide feedback if requested.

Website Insights for Interview Success

A thorough review of the company's website provides essential context, including an understanding of the company's product landscape, strategic direction (mission, vision, values), recent achievements (news/updates), and cultural signals. This information allows you to articulate tailored contributions and ask insightful questions that demonstrate strategic thinking. It's about showing that you're not just seeking a job but also grasp the ecosystem you aim to lead within.

Check for Skeletons in the Closet

You can learn about the company culture by searching your contacts for individuals who have worked there. Then, ask them directly about their experiences. People are often refreshingly honest when they have had a positive or negative experience, so listen carefully and read between the lines.

Research Your Interviewers

Before your interview, ask the recruiters for a list of the individuals you'll be meeting. Use LinkedIn to discover shared connections and work history, then prepare tailored questions for each person. This not only shows you've taken the time to learn about them, but also reveals whether they've extended the same courtesy to you through their responses.

Interviewers often experience "interview fatigue" from speaking with multiple candidates. Signs of this can include arriving late, seeming unprepared, or appearing distracted. Doing your homework allows you to identify who genuinely interests you and, importantly, who is genuinely interested in you. If you don't feel a connection with someone, especially if they'd be a critical relationship like your potential hiring manager, trust your instincts. It might indicate that this isn't a role where you'll thrive under their guidance. Remember, people always reveal who they are through their actions and words; your job is to observe and listen.

Master Your Presentation

We've all endured boring, disconnected presentations. To avoid this, rehearse enough that you can confidently continue speaking your truth to your audience, no matter what happens. A presentation offers your audience a chance to see you as a leader, so rehearse the impact you want to convey about yourself.

Many excellent resources exist for improving communication. I'm particularly fond of Vinh Quang Giang's tip, which he shared on Instagram. He suggests practicing your interview presentation and recording it on video. The next day, review your recording in three different ways. He calls this process "record and review."

1. **Listen only** (with sound up and video off) to evaluate your vocal quality.

2. **Watch only** (with sound off) to assess your body language and facial expressions.

3. **Transcribe the video,** including filler words (such as "ums" and "ahs"); then review the transcript with a red pen to mark these distractions.

Share Lessons You've Learned

If appropriate, try to mention lessons you've learned that reflect on how you've grown and, specifically, how you would apply what you learned in future roles. This demonstrates self-awareness and a commitment to continuous improvement. For example, "While the redesign was highly successful, I learned the importance of involving engineering earlier to ensure seamless implementation. This is a best practice I will carry forward to future projects."

Mastering Situational Interview Questions: The STAR Technique

Get ready for situational questions, as they're a staple in most interviews. These prompts ask you to pull from your past experiences, providing a concrete example of how you handled a specific scenario. For instance, an interviewer might ask, "Tell me about a time you had a conflict with a coworker and the resolution," or "Describe a mistake you made and how you addressed it."

Many tech companies assign different interviewers to probe for specific qualities they value in leaders, such as motivation, drive, creativity, innovation, experience level, leadership potential, and cultural fit. After your interview, the panel will debrief, with each person sharing their insights on your responses to these behavioral questions. Typically, a moderator, often the hiring manager, will then invite additional feedback on your strengths as a candidate.

The STAR interview technique is a structured method used by job candidates to answer behavioral and situational interview questions. It stands for:

S - Situation: Describe the context or background of the situation you are about to discuss. Provide enough detail for the interviewer to understand the scenario.

T - Task: Explain your role and what your responsibility or goal was in that situation. What needed to be accomplished?

A - Action: Detail the specific steps you took to address the situation or complete the task. Focus on *your* individual contributions, using "I" statements.

R - Result: Describe the outcome of your actions. What was achieved? What did you learn? Quantify results if possible (e.g., "reduced costs by 15%," "improved customer satisfaction by X points").

Development Dimensions International developed the STAR method in 1974. It's widely used because past behavior is a strong indicator of future performance. This technique helps interviewers assess your actual skills and competencies by providing a clear, evidence-based understanding of how you've handled real-world challenges. For you, it offers a logical framework to share impactful stories and clearly demonstrate key competencies.

While STAR focuses on your Task, the SOAR method (Situation, Obstacle, Action, Result) takes a slightly different approach by emphasizing the challenges or obstacles you faced. Regardless of the specific acronym, the key is to have well-prepared stories from your experience, and these frameworks provide a powerful way to narrate your experiences. Here are some examples of how you could tell your story using the STAR method.

The Situation You Encountered

The interviewer wants to understand the context, not your entire history with the project or politics of your least employer. Keep the situation description brief—one or two sentences should suffice. For example, if asked about a time you achieved a seemingly impossible design goal, you might say: "Our company was launching a new mobile app with an aggressive deadline and a limited budget. My challenge was leading the design team to create a user-friendly and visually appealing app within these constraints."

Or, if the question focuses on a time when you had to influence stakeholders regarding a design direction, you could say: "We were developing a new software-as-a-service platform, and the product team initially envisioned a feature set that I believed would compromise the overall user experience."

The Task You Performed

The task is the specific design challenge you were responsible for, not just the overall project goal. This is your chance to establish your direct ownership and set the stage for your actions. For example, "As VP of Product Design, I was tasked with redesigning the user onboarding flow to reduce churn and increase feature adoption by 20% within six months." This clearly defines your responsibility within the broader context.

The Action You Took

This is your opportunity to demonstrate executive-level thinking and leadership, highlighting your strategic approach and impact on the design organization and the broader business. For example, "This involved defining the new user journey, overseeing the UX research, and directing the visual design and prototyping efforts."

The Results You Achieved

When discussing your achievements, always quantify them using metrics that resonate with business leaders. Think about how your work impacted key objectives like increased conversion rates, improved user engagement, reduced development costs, or higher customer satisfaction.

Your metrics can be hard data, such as "I increased daily active users by 15% and average session duration by 20%." But don't overlook qualitative, "soft" metrics like enhanced brand recognition, positive media coverage, or improved customer feedback. For instance, you could say, "I streamlined internal processes, leading to greater cohesion within the design team and more effective cross-functional collaboration."

Highlight the long-term effects of your decisions. Did you foster a more user-centric culture within the company? Did a pattern library you created become a key brand differentiator, attracting top design talent? Demonstrating this long-term vision is crucial for showcasing executive potential.

To help you tell your own career narrative using these methods, here are some one-sentence SOAR statements taken from a resume and reframed as answers to situational interview questions, incorporating the STAR method.

Example 1: Focusing on Team Leadership and Process Improvement

SOAR: "Enhanced design quality and consistency, cutting revisions by 25% via a new, systemized design process."

STAR: "Recognizing the inconsistent quality of our design output, I initiated a comprehensive audit of our existing design processes. This involved interviewing designers, product managers, and engineers to pinpoint bottlenecks and areas for improvement. Based on these findings, I led the development and implementation of a new design system, including standardized UI components, a clear style guide, and a robust design review process. This improved the consistency and quality of our designs and increased team efficiency by 25%, as measured by the reduction in design revisions."

Example 2: Focusing on Cross-Functional Collaboration and Influence

SOAR: Secured executive approval for an app redesign that boosted daily active users by 15% in three months.

STAR: "To address the declining user engagement on our mobile app, I collaborated closely with the product and engineering teams to define clear success metrics and prioritize user needs. I presented user research data and design prototypes to key stakeholders, advocating for a complete redesign of the app's navigation and user interface. This required navigating competing priorities and building consensus across different departments. Ultimately, I secured executive buy-in for the proposed changes, which resulted in a 15% increase in daily active users within three months of launch."

Example 3: Focusing on Strategic Vision and Innovation

SOAR: Led a brand refresh, developing a new visual identity and messaging that increased brand awareness by 10% (via social media engagement).

STAR: "To elevate our brand's visual identity and position us as a leader in the market, I spearheaded a comprehensive brand refresh initiative. This involved conducting market research, analyzing competitor branding, and collaborating with a cross-functional team to develop a new visual language and messaging framework. I then presented this vision to the executive team, securing their approval and the necessary resources to implement the changes across all our platforms. This initiative modernized our brand image and contributed to a 10% increase in brand awareness, as measured by social media engagement."

Example 4: Focusing on Data-Driven Decision Making

SOAR: Increased our e-commerce conversion rates by 20% in six months by establishing an A/B testing framework and iteratively refining designs based on our test result data.

STAR: "Faced with optimizing conversion rates on our e-commerce platform, I implemented a data-driven approach to design. I established a robust A/B testing framework and worked with the analytics team to identify key areas for experimentation. I then led the design team in developing multiple design variations for these areas, iteratively testing and refining them based on user feedback and performance data. This data-driven approach resulted in a 20% improvement in conversion rates within six months."

With your interview complete and, hopefully, a compelling offer on the table, the journey isn't quite over. The final crucial stage involves navigating the offer and understanding how to negotiate effectively. This is your opportunity to ensure the compensation package and overall terms align with your values and expectations as an executive leader in the tech industry. Know that an initial offer is just that: a place to begin talking in detail about what would make you happy and feel valued about joining the company as an executive.

NEGOTIATING YOUR TOTAL COMPENSATION PACKAGE

The "total compensation package" represents an organization's complete value proposition—a strategic blend designed to attract, motivate, and retain top-tier leadership. Think beyond the regular paycheck; this encompasses a range of components that reflect your significant impact and long-term alignment with the company's success. You might already know this, but it's always a good idea to review all your options when discussing your overall compensation package. Your peers in the executive suite take it for granted that an offer is just the starting point. This negotiation process is, in fact, an early test of your leadership skills, revealing how effectively you'll advocate for what makes you happy and content in your new role.

A substantial portion of the overall earnings potential for executive roles often lies in short-term incentives (STIs) or bonuses. These performance-driven cash rewards are tied to achieving key milestones, such as hitting revenue targets, boosting user growth, or launching a critical product. Sign-on

Bonuses are one-time payments used to attract candidates to join the company. If you need to move for the role, the company may provide compensation for moving expenses in the form of Relocation Assistance.

Long-term incentives (LTIs) often have the potential for significant wealth creation in tech. These tools link your success directly to the company's long-term trajectory, typically vesting over several years. Common forms you might encounter include stock options, which grant the right to purchase company stock at a predetermined price (the grant price) for a specific period. You benefit if the stock price appreciates above this price. You may also gain access to restricted stock units (RSUs), which are essentially grants of company stock you receive over time. Occasionally, you may also encounter performance shares, where the number of shares you receive depends on achieving ambitious long-term goals. Equity isn't just about a future payout; it's about aligning your interests directly with the company's expansion and potential for a significant exit event like an IPO or acquisition. Here are a few more subsections of the total compensation package that you might see:

Benefits

These are the non-cash components of the package and can include:

- **Health Insurance.** Comprehensive medical, dental, and vision coverage.

- **Retirement Plans.** Contributions to 401(k) or other pension plans.

- **Life Insurance.** Company-provided or subsidized life insurance policies.

- **Disability Insurance.** Short-term and long-term disability coverage.

- **Paid Time Off.** Generous vacation, sick leave, and holidays.

Severance Package

Terms outlining compensation and benefits if your executive employment is terminated under certain circumstances.

Perks

These are additional benefits or privileges often provided to executives, which can include:

- Company Car or Car Allowance.

- Executive Coaching or Development Programs.

- Financial Planning Services.

- Club Memberships.

- Executive Health Programs.

As a creative leader in the tech world, wealth creation may or may not be your primary goal. But it's a part of your business, so you may as well consider it as carefully as you do your primary objectives to lead a kickass design group. Money is a form of exchange; the more you have, the more choices you create. So, when the offer comes in, take the time to understand the company's equity structure, vesting schedule, and option pricing. Don't hesitate to negotiate for a fair equity stake that aligns with your contributions and the company's potential. It's the key to unlocking true, long-term wealth. You don't need me to tell you how to negotiate; there are many excellent sources. The two I refer to most frequently are "How Not to Bomb Your Offer Negotiation" by Haseeb Qureshi[5] and "15 Rules for Negotiating a Job Offer" by Deepak Malhotra, Professor of Business Administration at Harvard Business School.[6]

Your Compensation Research

It's smart to research salary ranges at comparable tech companies so you understand your potential compensation. Focus on organizations similar in size, location, and industry. When conducting this research, use reputable salary websites like Glassdoor, Salary.com, and Levels.fyi. Leverage your professional network to gather qualitative insights into compensation for similar design leadership roles. Contact design leaders and executives you know through LinkedIn, industry events, or your existing connections. While they may not share exact salary figures, they can provide valuable context about typical compensation structures, the balance between salary and equity at different company stages, and what might be considered a competitive package. For instance, a contact who is a VP of Design at a larger, established e-commerce company might tell you that total compensation for a Director-level role typically

---

[5] Qureshi, Haseeb. "How Not to Bomb Your Offer Negotiation." *Haseeb Qureshi*. Accessed May 5, 2025. https://haseebq.com/how-not-to-bomb-your-offer-negotiation/

[6] Malhotra, Deepak. "15 Rules for Negotiating a Job Offer." April 1, 2014. Accessed May 5, 2025. https://hbr.org/2014/04/15-rules-for-negotiating-a-job-offer

includes a significant base salary and a smaller percentage of RSUs. Conversely, a design leader at a smaller startup might emphasize a lower base salary but a more substantial equity grant to attract leadership talent.

Understanding Company Stage and Equity Considerations

The stage of a tech company—whether it's a nascent startup, a rapidly expanding growth-stage enterprise, or an established industry leader—significantly shapes its compensation philosophy. Startups often present a compelling trade-off: a potentially lower base salary balanced by the allure of substantial equity opportunities. It is crucial to articulate your understanding of this dynamic and express your willingness to have "skin in the game" if this aligns with your long-term financial aspirations and your conviction in the company's vision.

However, if the offered salary reflects a significant reduction, carefully weigh the potential benefits of the equity against your immediate financial needs. Before entering negotiations, define your absolute minimum and maximum acceptable salary range, ensuring you remain realistic while firmly advocating for the value you bring and considering all aspects that are important to you. I experienced this firsthand when I chose to take a salary reduction to join Yahoo when stock options constituted a significant part of their total compensation. Ultimately, that equity proved to be far more valuable in the long run than my initial salary.

Negotiation Communication

First, focus on showcasing your skills and suitability for the role. Once you've established mutual interest, it is appropriate to discuss compensation. Avoid discussing salary too early in the interview; allow it to arise naturally. Be prepared to be flexible, but do not compromise on your non-negotiables. There may be room to negotiate various aspects of the package (such as trading a slightly lower base salary for more equity), so be sure to pursue this if there's something specific you're looking for.

Don't be afraid to walk away from an offer. If you have researched and know your bottom line, be prepared to decline an offer if it doesn't meet your needs and expectations. It's better to walk away from a bad deal than to accept a role that undervalues you. Equally, be ready to negotiate if securing that additional piece would make all the difference between starting there over the moon versus feeling resentful; go for it.

One of my most empowering moments was when I asked for a salary adjustment, and the hiring manager told me he was only authorized to go to a certain amount and that he'd have to ask the CEO to approve the increase. I said, "Thank you for looking into that for me. I look forward to hearing from you." They agreed to the salary increase, and I joined the company feeling valued by a company prepared to go the extra mile to ensure my happiness.

Document Everything

When the offer letter arrives, document all aspects of the compensation package, including salary, benefits, equity, and perks. If any verbal agreements are made during the negotiation process, confirm them in writing to avoid misunderstandings later. Please review it carefully before accepting, and if you have any questions, have a lawyer read it over. If you have any qualms, have them explain the legal contract. Then, go out and celebrate your success and prepare for the next chapter in your leadership journey.

Now that you're equipped with the strategies to level up and secure that coveted leadership position, let's turn our attention to someone who has already navigated this path with remarkable success. We'll explore the journey of Phil Clevenger and uncover the insights that have propelled him to the pinnacle of design leadership. In my interview with him, Phil generously shared his story and invaluable experiences from a distinguished career as both a designer and an executive design leader at some of the world's most renowned tech companies.

EXECUTIVE INSIGHT WITH PHIL CLEVENGER

As the Vice President of Product Experience at DocuSign, he leads a team of over 150 professionals and oversees the design and development of new experiences across the company's product portfolio. Before his role at DocuSign, Phil spent 17 years at Adobe, where he was the Senior Director of Experience Design for Adobe's Experience Cloud. He co founded Cooperating Systems Inc. and collaborated with renowned designer Kai Krause at the Applied Innovations Research Lab. Phil's career began at MetaCreations, where he played a pivotal role in the company's growth from a startup to a public limited company. With his extensive experience and strategic vision, Phil continues to shape the future of digital experiences.

What lessons did you learn from your early management roles that have informed your leadership style today?

My design career began at MetaCreations Corp. when Kai Krause hired me for my ability to be a rational influence, not my design skills! Kai hired me to be his lynchpin of sanity in a sea of startup craziness and went on to teach me everything I know. He was very generous with his wisdom, knowledge, and skills. The things that he taught me are things that I still use every day!

> *"I wanted to sit in a corner*
> *and design beautiful things."*

During my ten years working with Kai, what began as an apprenticeship quickly transformed me from a junior designer to a senior designer, then a design director, and finally a Vice President of software development. I was responsible for engineering, design, web development, and QA. To be honest, at this altitude, I felt out of my league and unwelcome by my new executive peers, who may have thought I rose too fast with Kai's sponsorship.

After MetaCreations, I co-founded a startup and, four years later, ended up at Adobe. I had consciously returned to individual design work and, at my interview, explicitly told the recruiters I did not want to manage. Rather, I wanted to sit in a corner and design beautiful things. And I did, designing the first versions of Adobe Lightroom, a product that still generates big revenue for Adobe to this day.

Adobe allowed me to do this for a year or three, but I was tapped for management again after a couple of years to lead a team in India for a special assignment. Here, I was allowed to split my time between managing and designing, but I soon realized that I couldn't do both. So, I backfilled my individual contributor design position and dedicated myself to my leadership mission with that team. What I quickly found out was that, this time, I very much liked managing people.

What advice would you give to aspiring managers who are concerned about losing their creative spark?

As a designer, I was necessarily very self-oriented, focusing on getting my designs approved, making solid supporting arguments, and ensuring I had delivered the very best I could. Everything was about me. It was a 24-hour cycle of worry and stress. When I transitioned to leadership, I appreciated the end of the relentless daily grind and the opportunity to focus on other people.

In India, I dove deeper into the lives of the people I managed. Many faced significant family pressure to pursue more traditional careers like medicine or engineering; breaking from that expectation could lead to familial disownment. Understanding their unique journeys helped me empathize with and support their professional growth.

This shift from self-focus to service was a significant turning point. It energized me and aligned with my career goals. These days, when individual contributors express concerns about transitioning to management, I advise them to approach the role with kindness and empathy; by focusing on supporting their team members, they'll find success.

What are the most significant challenges you've faced in building and maintaining cohesive teams, particularly as a leader of larger cross-functional organizations?

I've led teams ranging from 1 to 150 people. One unexpected challenge I've found is simply remembering everyone's names. Team members take that very personally, and rightly so. In cases of error, my first approach has been to handle it like you would a cocktail party faux pas: apologize sincerely, correct the name, and move on. Even then, it's not always enough; it's much better to develop a real discipline of memory before problems arise.

When leading multi-function teams, team names/identities are also important. At DocuSign, I occasionally referred to our organization as the 'design team' since it reflects the collective focus of our work and my own discipline of origin. This, too, can be perceived as exclusionary or dismissive of specific roles that aren't explicitly mentioned. This is entirely understandable, and I've made a conscious effort to be more inclusive in my language.

My team at DocuSign is a diverse group of professionals, including Product Designers, User Researchers, Design Operations Specialists, Program Managers, Content Strategists, Developer Content Creators, User Help Writers, QAs, and Researchers. We work across DocuSign hubs in San Francisco, Seattle, and Chicago, as well as remotely across the US and Europe.

Despite my decades of experience and validation, impostor syndrome has dogged me every single day. This was particularly fraught the first time I was charged with leading a non-design team as Director at Adobe, when the Research team was placed under my supervision. This team consisted of individuals with PhDs and specialized knowledge, which absolutely made me feel like an impostor. I was concerned that this arrangement would be detrimental to their career progression, as I didn't have the expertise to mentor them effectively.

To alleviate these concerns, I reminded myself of organizational leaders like Barack Obama, who are successful despite not being experts in every field. They rely on their cabinets and staff to provide specialized knowledge, while they focus on making informed judgments.

I recalled that my mentor Kai Krause had hired me based on exactly that—my judgment skills—which helped me feel more confident in my ability to lead the research team. I sought out team members who were friendly and constructive and worked with them to make decisions.

This approach proved successful, and I became more comfortable leading teams outside of my own area of expertise. During the remainder of my time at Adobe, and especially when I joined DocuSign as Vice President of product experience, I was able to effectively manage multiple teams responsible for functions that I didn't have a background in.

Back to impostor syndrome itself, another part of my practice here is this: When the syndrome kicks in, and I am feeling insecure, I recall all the insanely smart and talented people who have believed in me and put me in the roles I have had. Surely those people cannot have been wrong time and time again! This is a helpful silent exercise that can calm even the most acute episode.

As a design leader, how do you advocate for the value of design within your organization, especially when faced with skepticism about its ROI?

Once you understand the business's objectives, you make sure that you have a real handle on those objectives, and then you build your design strategy to meet those objectives.

Here's an example. I've led the design of software-as-a-service (SaaS) products at DocuSign and Adobe. SaaS products aim to provide specific solutions to specific industry or niche needs, but the components of those solutions are frequently highly vertical, tightly bound, and poorly integrated.

One of Adobe's SaaS business objectives was to break apart their vertical product components into services to build a single bespoke environment, providing better functionality for customers and more flexibility for sales, with the ultimate objective being to increase revenue and create a stronger competitive advantage.

With that business objective in mind, our experience design objectives would be to improve the customer experience to match the specific needs of each customer and to reduce the learning curve for users with a frictionless user experience.

To accomplish this, we had to create more than just a design system, but what I call an experience delivery system that could get its arms around all of that by providing collections of standards, components, and meta-components that would enable the broader cross-functional team to deliver experiences that were as nimbly composable as the emerging back end, and that were easily navigable by end users no matter what set of features were being delivered.

A comprehensive experience delivery system like this is not the kind of thing that a business would ask for, but it's the kind of thing that user experience design teams know and need to do in order to accomplish the stated business goals. So, I would prioritize this experience delivery system in our design strategy sheet and set up our objectives and milestones accordingly.

What role did executive buy-in and engagement play in the effectiveness of your OKR process?

The time it took to create executive OKRs (Objectives and Key Results are a goal-setting framework that helps organizations define and track their most important outcomes), team OKRs, et cetera, and then do the laddering up and down for alignment has been, in my experience, incredibly time-consuming and in the end not as helpful to design as one would hope. I understand the purpose and the value of the concept, but the execution is where I have seen this falter and fail. One needs to work with all the cross-functional partners and teams to get these things done quickly, efficiently, and firmly so that teams can continue to execute within a stable framework. DocuSign was pretty good at this.

How does the shift from a startup to a public company impact the overall culture and priorities of a design team?

There's a significant difference between a company before and after it goes public. When I started my career with Kai Krause and MetaCreations, it was largely about pursuing projects we found exciting and trusting that the money would follow, and it usually did.

However, after going public, the focus shifted dramatically. As a public company like DocuSign or Adobe, the focus is on aggressive growth and maximizing returns for shareholders. With industry consolidation and other factors, the emphasis on financial performance has become even stronger. Our pre-IPO bespoke/high-touch/from-the-hip way of working no longer worked for the post-IPO context.

How crucial is executive sponsorship in fostering a thriving design organization within a tech company? Can you provide examples of how effective sponsorship can make a tangible difference?

Design's standing within a company can change as leadership evolves. I was lucky to work for a number of outstanding leaders at Adobe over my seventeen years there. They hired me, understood the value I brought, and they were my direct line to the CEO. My oxygen supply.

Over time, as these leaders retired or moved on, the political tenor understandably evolved, and I found myself without their support. Without oxygen. New leadership may not understand design's role in SaaS, and the work environment can shift. If people don't know you or your value, you spend time educating them, proving yourself all over again. That's why I emphasize always building relationships along the way and maintaining strong connections within and across your organization.

What strategies did you use to effectively communicate the importance of design spending to finance and senior leadership?

Once I became a senior director at Adobe, I oversaw discretionary spending on travel, compensation increases, recruiting, team-building events, etc. Occasionally, I needed to request additional funds from finance or my superiors for specific purposes. However, I maintained primary control over my team's accounting system and projections.

*"If people don't know you or your value,
you spend time educating them, proving yourself
all over again."*

What are some more effective strategies for allocating resources in product development, beyond the simple ratio approach?

What's the right ratio of design to product and engineering? It's often the first question asked by executives trying to get a handle on resourcing allocation. Logical on its face, but I have rarely seen this conversation and its necessary investigations bear real fruit.

In some cases, it's like being summoned to the Wicked Witch's throne room and being sent to find her broomstick. Simply a tactic to kick the can down the road.

Some leaders do ask in good faith. But more often than not, even after bringing back data and numbers, it doesn't matter. I have presented recommendations, only to hear, "Well, what does company X do? Company Y? Get more research on industry practices!" It's a flawed conversation from the start, relying on good faith that isn't always there.

The ideal situation is when discussions about resources are transparent across engineering, design, and product management teams. This allows everyone to sit down together and discuss the specific needs and requirements for a project. Once we have a clear understanding of the scope, the necessary resources, including the budget, can be allocated.

That said, there is an answer, in my opinion, if it wants to be heard: First, I don't favor a fixed design-to-engineering ratio because engineering often involves backend work that doesn't directly impact design. It makes more sense to look at the ratio of designers to feature-level product managers, start with a 1:1 assumption, and adjust from there as discovery warrants. I have too often seen cases where a lone designer is tasked with serving a dozen or more PMs and then bears the brunt of bottleneck complaints.

How do you measure and assess team performance, and what steps do you take to address any shortcomings?

When working with limited resources, I focused on training, promoting, or replacing underperforming team members.

To maximize efficiency, I ensured everyone was operating at their best. If someone wasn't, I took decisive action to address the issue. I was always on the lookout for sources of inefficiency and opportunities for improvement. If someone couldn't be trained up, I would look to replace them with a more suitable candidate. The goal was to maintain a high-performing team, avoid reaching a crisis point, and get HR involved with a transition plan to move them out within 90 days.

Mostly, I know I have a kick-ass design team because people will tell me so. Successful partnerships generate gratitude and appreciation, and Eng or PM folks will not hesitate to reach out and let me know. Positive impact is the goal.

In this context, it's important to look at how kickass teams are evaluated. Individuals often feel pressured to constantly ship products to be seen as valuable. I evaluate design teams based solely on the quality of their work and their ability to build positive relationships. These two factors are equally important. If I hear positive feedback about my team's collaboration with other departments and their product contributions, that's a good sign. And if I see high-quality work and strong relationships, I'm satisfied.

I think back to my days at MetaCreations and the incredible team we built. We inspired each other to be our best. We created a collaborative workspace where we could easily see and learn from each other's work. We were always pushing each other to new heights. But the secret sauce—the real magic—was our ability to fail together. We could try new things, make mistakes, and learn from them without fear of judgment. That kind of freedom is invaluable and absolutely makes for a kickass team.

What do you believe are the most significant challenges and opportunities facing designers today, compared to the past?

Things have changed significantly since the early days of design. Back then, we had to manually anti-alias text and deal with complex workflows involving floppy disks and remote localization processes. Hell, my first UI design work was done around a table with pencils and a roll of butcher paper. Today, tools like Canva and Figma Automator make the whole process so much more streamlined.

While modern designers have access to powerful tools, the creative freedom we enjoyed in the 90s and early 2000s has been largely replaced by established conventions and patterns. Newer designers often have a more formulaic approach, relying heavily on established guidelines. UX design curricula are often formulaic and lack classical design fundamentals.

When my team needs innovation or a fresh perspective, I look for designers who are relentlessly positive and capable of thinking outside the box. These individuals are often not as common today, especially among those coming from accelerated boot camps.

While patterns and conventions are valuable, they shouldn't be applied blindly. True innovation requires a willingness to challenge the status quo and explore new possibilities.

What's the impact on design when 'done' is better than perfect?

When 'done is better than perfect,' and it usually is, user research often takes a backseat. Companies may cut corners in areas like user testing to meet deadlines instead of relying on assumptions or small sample sizes. Additionally, younger researchers might use generic scripts or questionnaires, leading to gaps in understanding. At one employer, the pressure to move quickly on a particular initiative quickly led to a severe downscaling of user research. In earlier days at MetaCreations, we had no research team, but we had the luxury of involving real users deeply in the development process throughout. This allowed us to gather valuable feedback and make informed design decisions. Today, user research often involves scripted interviews or usability tests, which can limit the depth of insights. This can lead to missed opportunities to improve the user experience or, worse, to making serious decisions based on poorly formed research.

How do you balance your creative aspirations with your responsibilities as a leader, and what role does mentorship play in this?

For me, the biggest reward as an executive leader is having far more impact on a broader scale than I ever did as an individual contributor.

Early in my Adobe career, there was a very, very talented senior designer who took a role as a director, and I asked him: "You're so talented, why would you waste your cycles on management?" He replied: "I'm still designing, I just have more and different tools at my disposal." That made quite an impression on me.

Executive leadership has been a tremendous liberation from being a "prisoner of me" to being focused on other people. I've worked hard and accomplished a lot, so it costs me nothing to elevate other people. I really like being able to shine a light on others to elevate them or give them opportunities. This is what I got in spades from my early mentor, Kai Krause. I've always considered it a part of my mission as a leader to pay that forward and impact individual careers.

Lastly, as an executive leader, there is a mindset shift that needs to occur. You need to free yourself of some of the fears you had earlier in your career. For example, I had to learn to stop worrying about whether I'm right or whether I'm the best, and to lean back a little bit, take it all in, listen hard, use my best judgment, delegate well, empower others, and move to the next thing.

"For me, the biggest reward as an executive leader is having far more impact on a broader scale than I ever did as an individual contributor."

What specific benefits can leaders derive from overcoming their fears and becoming skilled public speakers?

While public speaking is not necessarily a requirement for successful career development, it sure does help! Many people struggle with public speaking, and I am often asked for advice about that.

One suggestion I have often found helpful is this: Look at video of your speaking engagement after the fact, and compare your internal experience to how you were perceived by your audience. Most people find that while they were feeling fearful, insecure, and even mortified as they spoke, the video instead shows someone who comes across as poised, calm, informed, and professional. That exercise alone can calm most fears!

Remember, your job really isn't to enjoy it. Most people do not, in fact. Your job is to deliver the message. It might not be fun, but it's just a role. Many of us fear we've made mistakes or come across poorly, but often our perception doesn't match reality. And the audience is always on your side.

Another crucial piece of advice: always speak from passion, not from notes. If you know your subject and are passionate and enthusiastic about it, there is no way to get unmoored during a presentation. Time and record your talk; rehearse and record it at least three times, refining and reducing your dependence upon notes each time. You will find your brain makes certain errors fairly consistently, and once you know that inventory of cul-de-sacs and wrong turns, recovery becomes natural and easy. When comparing good talks to great talks, the salient difference is almost always here: rehearse, observe, refine, and speak from passion. Ditch those speaker notes!

What advice would you give to aspiring creative leaders who are facing challenges in balancing their personal and professional lives?

As an executive design leader, your role is simply to fulfill the responsibilities of your position. Don't get caught up in whether you enjoy a particular task; focus on completing it and moving on to the next. Your job is just a role you're playing, and that's all it is. Discard fear. Embrace play. Don't take anything too personally. Keep calm and carry on. You're paid well to do the work, so do it. Then, at the end of the day and at the end of the week, set it aside and do all the other things. Be present with your family, play with your dogs, jump out of airplanes, do yoga and meditate, travel, eat, drink, and be merry. Life is short—enjoy every minute!

CHAPTER 2

How to Keep the Top Job

THE HIGH STAKES WORLD OF EXECUTIVE LEADERSHIP

Welcome to the rarefied air of executive design leadership. As a former Chief Design Officer, I've navigated this territory's exhilarating highs and demanding lows. It takes you away from the people you know, like, and trust, away from practicing your discipline and craft, and away from managing directly to a place that relies on projecting your value and having an impact through influence. Being an executive is lonely. Most of your time will be spent in back-to-back meetings with leaders who don't speak your language but expect you to speak theirs.

You will pore over spreadsheets, endlessly recruit and interview prospective new hires, conduct and write performance reviews, present to executives and other scary dudes, and respond to urgent and essential requests from on high. If you let it, it becomes a world where your time is not your own, and you are in a permanent state of context switching.

Yet, this is a rare, privileged position that others would kill to have. You now compete head-on for time, attention, and resources with exceptionally talented experts who will move states, countries, or continents to work in tech and receive life-changing financial rewards, making work at this level a full-contact sport. Others constantly scrutinize your performance during formal performance reviews, which could be as frequent as every quarter. Having consecutive reviews that merely "meet expectations," you could find yourself on a performance improvement plan. All of this makes it worthwhile to ask yourself if you really still want a job as an executive design leader.

The Mindset of Business Leaders vs. Designers

Business leaders focus on solving problems and fixing things. The work is verbal, analytical, and orderly in reading, writing, and computation, and it involves primarily left-brain thinking. They likely have a value-based education, where they were taught to measure their worth by collecting hard skills in business operations, marketing, financial strategy, quantitative analysis, etc.

As a designer who creates, modifies, repairs, or experiments, you live in the broader world of creation, expansion, and process flow. You act from the heart to create change and realize potential. It makes you adept at right-brain thinking. Your education was likely geared toward creating a portfolio of work to demonstrate your skills.

While not possessing a Master of Business Administration (MBA) doesn't disqualify you from executive leadership in tech, the creative behavior, beliefs, and communication skills that got you into the senior leadership team may not be enough to succeed in the long term without additional investment in financial education and learning how to communicate the value of your organization's output to the business bottom line.

THRIVING AS A DESIGN LEADER IN THE EXECUTIVE ARENA

The tech industry, while highly coveted, is notoriously volatile. As an executive, you'll witness rapid shifts in valuations driven by public sentiment, breakneck innovation, and the sheer economic power of Big Tech. You'll see the impact of downturns and be exposed to the industry's unpredictability. Yet, despite this, you'll find countless individuals, yourself included, drawn to work in this space because you recognize the magnetic pull of tech: the promise of shaping the future through design, the rapid growth potential, the long-term rewards of mastering a constantly evolving landscape, and the enduring payoffs of a dynamic career match the initial allure. As Ajay Thakur, head of cognitive computing at Uber puts it in our interview in Chapter 8, "The challenge of problem-solving keeps me coming back for more. There's a unique thrill in tackling complex technical issues and finding innovative solutions."

POWER, WEALTH, AND THE PRICE OF SUCCESS

As an executive, your success hinges on mastering many roles while competing for resources, access to power, and projects that will embolden your team's influence and impact. Suppose your career success is built on a strong portfolio, excellent design leadership, and hard work; this may not be enough to sustain you as an executive. The financial stakes in tech are incredibly high for both you and the company you work for. You will be expected to perform at the highest level, but you'll also have the potential to receive life-changing generational wealth.

"What got you here won't get you there."
Executive leadership coach Marshall Goldsmith

When your annual compensation breaches the seven-figure threshold, a mere starting point for tech executives, the driving forces shift. People change when you acquire a taste for fine wines, expensive cars, the best schools, five-star+ luxury hotels, Michelin-starred meals, ski-in, ski-out homes in the best resorts, and don't forget the bragging rights. "I'm sorry I was late for dinner. I was waiting for a driver to pick up my Ferrari and drive it 300 miles to Los Angeles for an engine tune-up." Or "I was amazed that the down payment on a new Lamborghini was only 10%. They make it so easy to preorder, so I did."

It's no longer just about passion; it's a cocktail of anxiety-laced ambition and greed you're pressured to conceal. Wealth accumulation is undeniably a potent intoxicant capable of reshaping even the most grounded individuals. If your lifestyle inflates in lockstep with your skyrocketing income, the pressure to maintain that momentum becomes a relentless, gnawing force. You're constantly measured against your peers at the executive table, and your perceived value is a battleground. Welcome to the shark tank, where survival hinges on demonstrating unwavering, quantifiable impact. The stakes are high, and the competition is fierce. It's a game where complacency is a death sentence, and only the most strategically astute thrive.

Landing the top design leadership role in tech is a significant achievement, but the journey doesn't end there. Sustaining that position requires a proactive and multifaceted approach. This chapter delves into the essential strategies for first surviving and then thriving in the executive design seat. In this section, we'll explore how to demonstrate your impact rapidly, build unshakeable relationships, remain at the forefront of innovation, articulate your vision with precision, and amplify your sphere of influence. We'll also discuss how to navigate inevitable shifts with resilience, deeply integrate with your company's ethos, safeguard your well-being, take decisive action when challenges arise, and effectively manage the emotional landscape that comes with high-stakes leadership. This is your guide to long-term success and continued impact at the highest level.

PROVE YOUR VALUE QUICKLY

Quantify Impact

Tech doesn't wait. You must swiftly pinpoint the business metrics that matter and align them to design KPIs that can map to measurable results. As a Chief Design Officer or equivalent, your first strategic move is identifying the precise business outcomes your design efforts will impact. We're talking about direct, measurable outcomes. Are you driving financial performance by optimizing conversion funnels? Fueling growth through increased user acquisition and sign-ups? Or solidifying user loyalty by elevating customer satisfaction (CSAT)? Knowing what the business goals are and deciding how to achieve them becomes your narrative for quantifying your team's impact—a data-backed story of design's strategic contribution.

Pick a North Star Project Goal

Crystallize your target for the project outcome into an unambiguous, measurable goal. We're talking about a concrete benchmark, like "boost new user task completion rates by 20% within the next quarter." This becomes a strategic declaration that your team rallies around. It's the North Star that aligns your team's efforts and provides a clear, data-driven definition of success. With this declaration, you track progress by ensuring every design decision contributes to achieving that defined target.

Establish Your Baseline

You need a baseline to compare the proposed project goal against the defined target. For example, if your objective is to elevate financial performance through a 15% conversion rate increase within six months, you must first understand the current conversion rate. This baseline measurement allows you to calculate the necessary monthly incremental growth, transforming a long-term goal into actionable, short-term milestones. Your role is not simply tracking progress; you're actively managing the trajectory, ensuring every design iteration directly contributes to closing the gap between the baseline and your ambitious target.

Leveraging Past Performance for Future Design

As an executive, you need to be able to predict and plan for challenges that might pop up in the future. It helps to have a historical understanding of what has and has not worked to move the business needle because of changes made to the customer experience. You might analyze product performance trends each quarter to extract strategic intelligence. For example, did a recent redesign correlate with a measurable uplift in customer growth, customer care costs, or subscriptions? Are there any seasonal or event-driven fluctuations impacting key metrics? By examining historical product performance data, you gain context, enabling you to set realistic user experience and data-informed targets. This proactive approach allows you to anticipate potential challenges and opportunities, moving beyond reactive adjustments to a strategic, predictive design methodology. As a design leader, you're not just observing the past but leveraging it to architect a more effective and resilient user experience.

Every business measures its results differently and at different times. Once you decide on the business objectives of strategic importance that your team can directly influence, you can set up research and reviews in a cadence that matches the business's pace. For example, user engagement metrics may require a weekly review, whereas measuring customer lifetime value may take more time and only need to be reviewed on a quarterly basis.

FORGE STRONG ALLIANCES

In executive leadership, allies are indispensable. Your success, and that of your team, hinges on these supportive relationships. Allies provide a vital safety net during challenging times, offering unwavering trust, encouragement, and a crucial sounding board for navigating complex situations.

Effective allies become partners in overcoming organizational hurdles, including political resistance and change management. This reciprocal support fosters a deeper understanding of each other's roles and the broader organizational landscape. While long-tenured leaders often possess established networks, those in new roles face the challenge of building rapport quickly. This period of relationship development can leave you exposed, as perception is paramount in leadership. Remember, it's often not solely your actions, but how others interpret and communicate them to others that shape your reputation.

Failing to cultivate alliances can lead to misperceptions and missed opportunities. If people are unaware of you or your value to the business, their ignorance can hinder your progress. Importantly, allies aren't confined to your immediate peers or superiors. Genuine alliances manifest as regular, informal, and unscheduled interactions. Building these relationships requires consistent effort and should be prioritized as highly as any other critical aspect of your leadership. These are not overnight creations; they are investments in your long-term success.

Elevate Your Visibility

Don't wait for an invitation—proactively position yourself and your team at the center of strategic discussions. If you report to a departmental head, such as in marketing or engineering, but aspire to influence the divisional level, bridge that gap. Ensure your insights reach the leaders shaping the overall business direction. I learned this firsthand at Yahoo, where I led the Media division of UED. Initially, a "dotted-line" matrixed reporting structure kept me from attending critical business meetings. (Matrixed reporting is where individuals report to more than one manager, and while they offer benefits like resource efficiency and flexibility, they also require careful management to mitigate potential challenges such as conflicting priorities and communication issues.)

Asking the general manager (GM) of Media if I could attend his extended staff meetings changed everything. He willingly agreed to include me at a weekly business unit meeting. This inclusion made our work visible and our contribution clear, and being part of early discussions for new projects helped bring alignment across all functions. Don't be afraid to reach out and build rapport with senior business leaders. Learn about their function, ask about their goals and how you can support them, align on process and collaboration, and share your wins. With their support, you both expand your professional influence and impact in the top job.

Cultivate Trust: Transparency, Accountability, Consistency

Trust is a delicate yet powerful force that hinges on your consistent demonstration of your reliability and integrity. It's earned through time and woven from threads of honesty, dependability, and respect. While easily fractured, nurtured trust forms the bedrock of meaningful relationships. You already understand this, and as an executive, you must extend this understanding upwards and laterally, securing your position through earned confidence.

To build this trust, be open and honest in every communication and action, own your decisions, and maintain a consistent leadership approach. For example, illuminate the goals of a redesign, the research driving it, and its direct impact on the business's bottom line. Share work in progress through inclusive design reviews with matrixed partners and extended stakeholders.

When roadblocks arise, don't retreat—address them head-on. Openly discuss challenges and detail the team's strategies for resolution. Emphasize the crucial role of data and user feedback, sharing positive and negative findings to demonstrate how they inform design iterations. Remember, business leaders typically operate in a realm of data and logic, not design intuition. This doesn't mean compromising design principles; it means translating them.

Reinforce trust through unwavering reliability. Deliver on your promises, set realistic expectations, and consistently meet deadlines. Establish transparent design processes, workflows, and handoffs, ensuring everyone—both within your team and external collaborators—clearly understands their roles, responsibilities, and accountability to the bottom line. Predictability is a cornerstone of business; it provides the stable platform upon which sustainable innovation and growth can be built. By upholding the tech cornerstones of innovation, agility, and predictable growth, you will solidify your reputation as a dependable and trustworthy leader.

STAY ON THE CUTTING EDGE

Continuously immersing yourself in emerging technologies and understanding their potential to drive innovation and create unparalleled user value is one way to be relevant and ensure you fulfill part of your mandate to shape the future.

If learning about business and tech is daunting, consider this an investment that will pay you huge dividends over time. Think of it as user research! Carve out time to engage with relevant content, follow influential figures, and subscribe to newsletters that concisely summarize key tech trends. Read earnings reports for the company, competitors, and the industry. Set news alerts for things you might do well to be up to speed on. Use AI tools to summarize things for you. Your efforts to broaden your knowledge will sharpen your business acumen and enable you to communicate effectively with fellow business leaders.

COMMUNICATE WITH CLARITY

As a senior leader, your communication needs to deliver maximum impact in minimal time to reach its mark. If you focus on every single iteration, user testing result, and pixel adjustment like this: "First, we explored this; then, we tried that; then, we discovered this..." your audience will struggle to understand the point of your story, not understand what you need from them, or whether they should even care. Learning to communicate succinctly is key. Sophie Hirst, ex-Google manager and founder of Workbaby, recommends using the 'Preview and Pause' framework to communicate with clarity. Here's an example: "We've finalized the core user flow for the app, and I'm ready to get your input on the key interaction for onboarding new users. I've narrowed it down to two approaches: one emphasizes speed, while the other emphasizes guided discovery. I will walk you through the key differences and their potential impact on user adoption. Is this the right level of detail for you right now, or would you prefer a high-level summary?"

Rather than overwhelm the audience with ephemeral information, you've set the stage, emphasized the key decision points, and paused to allow the audience to steer the conversation. They might say, "Great, guide us through the two approaches," or, "Just tell us the main points—which one do you recommend and why?" Regardless, you've respected their time, showcased your strategic thinking, and positioned yourself as someone who can communicate effectively at any level. This succinct communication structure works like this:

Preview

Context: Set the stage for your audience about what you are discussing. "We've finalized the core user flow for the app."

Intent: Explain why you are sharing this information. "I'm ready to get your input on the key interaction for onboarding new users."

Summary: Provide an outline of what you will discuss with them and what you need from them. "I've narrowed it down to two approaches: one emphasizes speed, while the other emphasizes guided discovery. I will walk you through the key differences and their potential impact on user adoption."

Pause

Signal: Pause for acknowledgment that your message is clear, and if you've given them choices, seek their input on how they'd like to direct the conversation. "Is this the right level of detail for you right now, or would you prefer a high-level summary?"

BE A PROBLEM SOLVER, NOT A PROBLEM BRINGER

You, your boss, and the executive team operate in a high-stakes environment where time is crucial. No one values having their plates overloaded with unresolved issues. For this audience, you can't simply highlight surface problems and not have a solution. Your role is to communicate vetted actionable solutions that enable swift decision-making, demonstrate your thought leadership, and allow executives to concentrate on strategic initiatives. For example, "Our rising acquisition costs and customer stagnant engagement signal onboarding friction. I've devised an A/B testing of an alternative onboarding sequence to increase user activation by 10% and lower acquisition costs by 5%. When can we meet to prioritize which strategy is most effective for driving growth?" Whether you are updating the project design, making requests, or raising concerns about a critical issue, the way you present a problem and a solution to executives can be created using the same outline. First, you identify the problem, propose a specific solution, quantify the intended impact, make a request, and set a feasible timeline. You can use this formula to meet your needs in any context. Here are three examples using the most common requests you will likely need to make of your boss or the executive team.

1.   Requesting a Design Review

The Problem: "The Phoenix project, which aims to increase user conversion by 20%, launches in two weeks. To mitigate launch risks, we need executive alignment on the final user flow."

The Solution: "A design review to present the final flow, key design decisions, and address any potential concerns, allowing for real-time feedback and ensuring we launch with full executive confidence."

The Ask: "A 60-minute calendar slot for me to present a concise overview focusing on the core user experience and its intended strategic impact."

The Timeline: "Hold the design review next week, make adjustments based on your feedback within 48 hours, and launch in two weeks."

The Impact: "Additionally, having a clear view of the design team's process will support a smoother launch, reduce post-launch adjustments, ensure strategic alignment, and contribute to the 20% conversion target."

2. Making a Headcount Request

Problem: "A 30% increase in product development requests is straining our design team, directly threatening upcoming launch timelines and potentially jeopardizing projected revenue streams."

Solution: "Hiring a senior UX designer and one visual designer will enhance our capability to meet these demands, speed up time-to-market, and capitalize on critical market opportunities."

The Ask: "I'm seeking your approval to recruit these two vital roles to ensure we can execute our product roadmap and meet our revenue targets."

The Timeline: "With expedited recruitment, we can onboard these new team members within two months, protecting our launch schedules and minimizing potential revenue loss."

The Impact: "This strategic headcount increase will accelerate revenue growth by ensuring timely product launches and capturing market share. Eliminating design bottlenecks and maintaining project momentum will reduce the risk of missed targets. Preventing burnout and fostering a high-performing design team will increase team efficiency and retention."

3. Reporting a Problem Affecting the Bottom Line

The Problem: "CSAT is down 15%, directly impacting customer retention and potentially revenue. We're experiencing a spike in churn tied to user frustration navigating the app."

The Solution: "Rapid user research has identified key navigational pain points. We've developed a plan for iterative design changes and targeted user testing to reverse this trend."

The Ask: "I need a review session with you to present our findings and secure resources for four weeks of increased user testing. This will enable us to validate our improvements and mitigate potential revenue loss swiftly."

The Timeline: "Initial fixes within two weeks, and ongoing testing for one month. We project a recovery in CSAT and a reduction in churn within the next quarter, directly protecting our revenue stream."

The Impact: "We are turning a customer pain point into a revenue protection opportunity. Addressing it promptly will reduce churn, increase customer lifetime value, and safeguard our market share."

This formula is a powerful way to communicate actionable plans with measurable outcomes. It helps executives make informed decisions swiftly, align design initiatives with critical business objectives, and showcase their value as strategic thought leaders. Don't be a gatekeeper—teach it to your direct reports, too!

ASK GOOD QUESTIONS AND ACT ON THE FEEDBACK

Many leaders avoid asking questions for fear of appearing weak in the eyes of those whose opinions of them matter—this is a mistake. Consider all the things a CEO has on their plate; they cannot have answers to everything. Instead, they rely on asking open strategic questions and actively gather feedback to build a complete picture of their business.

When you ask open-ended questions with genuine curiosity, as you might see done in a usability test, you learn a lot about the other person, and they will feel their information is important and valued, making them feel heard. In tech, powerful questions are better known as "strategic inquiry" and follow a pattern of being open-ended. They are asked with genuine curiosity always start with "How" or "What."

- **"What"** questions encourage the exploration of possibilities, options, and perspectives. For example,

"What challenges are you facing?" or "What could be done differently?"

- **"How"** questions invite the exploration of processes, methods, and approaches. For instance, "How can we improve this?" or "How did you arrive at that conclusion?"

Unlike "Yes/No" questions, which confirm basic facts, "How" or "What" questions lead to deeper, more engaging conversations that foster collaboration.

Asking "Why" questions can be helpful, but may also put people on the defensive; they might feel interrogated or that they need to justify their actions. For instance, "Why did you do that?" can be received as being confrontational.

When a question is concise, between 8 and 12 words, the person you are asking can focus on forming a response, rather than trying to decipher a complex sentence. This reduces cognitive load, increases focus, reduces stress, fosters connection, and reduces bias in the answer. Here are some examples of powerful questions you might use to gather feedback on your team.

- What observations do you have about the design team's performance?

- Where do you see the biggest opportunities for design to elevate our product strategy?

- How well do you feel our design decisions are contributing to key product metrics?

- Where do you see opportunities for design to drive even greater value for the product?

- How clear are our design team's handoffs to engineering from your perspective?"

- How well are design insights integrating into our product roadmap and prioritization?

- What's one area where our design team could improve its collaboration with the product team for greater impact?

- What unique strengths do individual designers on my team bring to your product initiatives?

Tip: Remember to act on the feedback you receive. This will demonstrate that you value the opinions of those around you and are willing to improve.

BUILD YOUR PERSONAL BRAND

There are many ways to enhance your profile and build your reputation as a thought leader. For example, I love seeing design leaders on LinkedIn celebrating their recent hire or sharing photos from a successful offsite or speaking engagement. Their presence shows confidence in themselves and their company; they are brand ambassadors generating excitement within the design community about the excellent work their teams are doing. It's a strategic move on many levels, especially when the market shifts or cuts need to be made. The more visible you are, the more personal recognition you achieve, the more perceived and actual value you create, and the harder it will be for your company to let you go compared to a design leader who has chosen to remain invisible.

Elevate Your Voice: Building Your External Brand

Don't assume other leaders know your value because you hold an executive title. Being visible within and outside the company is crucial. Go ahead and seek out speaking opportunities at industry events, publish articles in relevant publications, and promote your work through social media and your website. Actively participate in online design communities by contributing to discussions and offering constructive feedback, rather than just self-promotion. You don't need to do it all; simply choose one activity and dedicate half an hour to it each week.

This strategic engagement nurtures relationships, increases your visibility, and solidifies your position as a leading voice in the design community. Building your brand outside the company only enhances your value within!

For instance, I still receive emails from students about my work for Apple researching patient record-keeping using mobile devices for nurse midwives in India. The moral of this story is clear: No matter how busy you become as an executive, make time to be a visible part of the community and share your thought leadership. You never know whom you might inspire to follow their passions and dreams, or where your next opportunity might come from.

Own Your Narrative: Proactive Communication of Achievements

Don't rely solely on performance reviews to communicate your achievements or assume your boss understands your career goals and ambitions. It's wise to maintain a running log of your accomplishments and take the time to quantify your impact whenever possible. Then, share your successes in appropriate settings, such as team meetings, presentations, one-on-ones, and performance reviews. This isn't bragging; it's a strategy to strengthen your position through effective communication by showcasing your value to the company.

The "Thank You Folder

Every time you receive a note from someone thanking you for something you did or said that helped them, put that note in a thank you folder! It boosts your morale and confidence on tough days. Here's an example of a note from my thank you folder:

> Hello Sally,
>
> Thank you for being my guiding light, encouraging me, and making me feel reasonable and more self-aware. You listened to me, and I felt very comfortable talking to you. Your positive vibe made me smile even while discussing my painful problem. Great coaches are hard to find. I am so thankful to have found one in you!

These notes and emails are a powerful pick-me-up, reminding you of your positive impact and value, thus reinforcing your confidence and motivation. And it provides concrete evidence for career advancement. Thank you notes offer invaluable, specific examples of your skills, achievements, and relationships for performance reviews, promotions, or job applications. Rather than just stating your contributions, you can use direct quotes to prove your value and make your accomplishments more credible.

Take Calculated Risks

Stepping out of your comfort zone is where professional growth happens. Leadership isn't just about maintaining the status quo; it's about pushing boundaries and navigating uncertainty. That might mean leading a high-stakes project, volunteering for an unfamiliar initiative, or even making a significant career pivot like moving from product design to product management, which is what Lynn Bacigulpo did, and you can read about in Chapter Six. Taking calculated professional risks lets you gain invaluable experience that cannot be learned in a predictable environment. These experiences not only enhance your skills but also build your resilience, adaptability, and strategic thinking— qualities essential for any effective leader. Ultimately, taking these calculated risks allows you to evolve, innovate, and prepare for even greater responsibilities.

EMBRACE CHANGE AND BOUNCE BACK

Organizational and Leadership Changes

I have witnessed tech companies invest heavily in building UX design teams and then, after three to four years, 'evolve' them into something quite different. Rapid growth may force a small, centralized design team to split into distributed teams aligned directly with business divisions, necessitating senior design leaders to oversee those teams. Alternatively, it could involve a downsizing decision to offshore all non-revenue-generating departments like UX Design, eliminating domestic teams and rebuilding in foreign countries with more affordable labor rates. Or it could be the addition of a new executive position, like chief product officer, that eliminates your executive role.

You can't make this stuff up, but it happens constantly in tech. All these changes are part of a business strategy to realign the company with the next wave of market shifts, buyouts, mergers, acquisitions, and technological innovations. That is the corporate prerogative—it's not personal. Still, it feels very personal when someone takes your laptop and badge, gives you some paperwork to sign, and walks you to your car. Or, somehow worse, you just get an email saying you've been let go. It is personal when you have invested in designing products and organizations, and risen to meet the demands of tech. But that's where learning how to bounce back comes in, and why the last section of this chapter (Take Action When Things Go Wrong) is probably the most critical piece of the book.

Building a sustainable user experience design team is complex, multilayered, incredibly rewarding, and sometimes utterly heartbreaking. By now, you understand how heart-wrenching it can be to build teams only to say goodbye or face being let go yourself. If this hasn't happened to you, that is wonderful, but unusual! There are a few things you can do to insulate yourself from these changes and help you bounce back if they do occur. Some things that are in your control to do include:

- Establish regular touchpoints with your counterparts in product, engineering, and marketing to foster open dialogue and a shared understanding of goals. This helps break down any silos by championing collaborative projects and creating cross-functional teams, demonstrating the power of unified efforts.

- I've said it once already, but remember to hone your ability to translate design impact into business value, using data and compelling narratives to ensure your relevance to the business.

- Practice articulating design's role in shaping the company's vision to become a trusted advisor to senior leadership.

- Anticipate rapid growth by developing scalable processes and flexible design systems. This ensures consistency and efficiency across all products and platforms. For a master class on creating a design system, check out how design director Colin Grigson implements this for the online remittance service Remitly in our interview at the end of this chapter.

UNDERSTAND AND LIVE THE COMPANY CULTURE

Successfully navigating your tech company's culture—its unspoken rules, ingrained habits, and core values—is paramount. This "shared DNA" isn't learned from a manual; it's absorbed through experience. Aligning with this culture is crucial for you to fit in, so do your research and actively seek out these subtle cues. This approach will give you a much deeper and more authentic understanding of the tech culture than any company handbook could provide.

> *"Culture is not just an expression of how your team works together; it's how they work together at their best."*
> *Reed Hoffman*

Meeting Dynamics

- **Decision-Making:** Who typically makes decisions in meetings? Is it the leader, or is there a strong emphasis on consensus? How are disagreements handled? Is it direct confrontation, or more indirect negotiation?

  o **Participation**: Who speaks up? Are junior employees encouraged to contribute, or do senior voices dominate? Is there a lot of cross-talk or do people wait their turn?

  o **Meeting Structure**: Are meetings tightly scheduled with agendas, or more free-flowing? Do they start and end on time?

  o **Humor and Banter**: What kind of jokes are common? Is there a lot of informal banter, or is the atmosphere strictly professional? This can reveal a lot about psychological safety and team cohesion.

- **Feedback Loops:** How is feedback given and received? Is it direct and immediate, or more formal and structured (e.g., quarterly reviews only)? Do people actively seek feedback or avoid it?

- **Documentation Habits:** Beyond email, where do teams store knowledge? Is it a wiki, Confluence, Google Docs, Notion, or something else? How organized and up-to-date is it? This indicates their approach to knowledge sharing and transparency.

- **Problem-Solving Approach:** When a problem arises, how do people react? Do they jump to solutions, analyze data, or seek input from many sources? Is there a "blame culture" or a "learn from mistakes" culture?

- **Use of Emojis/GIFs:** In informal communication tools like Slack, observe the frequency and type of emojis or GIFs used. This can signal the level of informality and playfulness in the culture.

  o **Response Times:** How quickly do people respond to messages (Slack, email, etc.)? This can indicate expectations around responsiveness and availability.

Observing Environment & Rituals (Beyond Physical Space)

- **Work-Life Integration:** How do people talk about their personal lives? Is there an expectation of always being "on," or is work-life balance genuinely encouraged and demonstrated?

- **Celebrations and Milestones:** How are successes, project launches, or personal milestones celebrated? Is it formal recognition, informal shout-outs, or team outings?

- **"Unwritten Rules":** Notice subtle cues. For example, is it acceptable to leave early on a Friday if your work is done? Do people eat lunch at their desks, or in a communal area? Are specific times of day considered "focus time" where interruptions are minimized?

- **Dress Code (Actual vs. Stated):** While you mentioned casual Friday, observe if the *stated* dress code aligns with what people actually wear on a day-to-day basis.

- **Perks and Benefits Utilization:** Do people actually use the gym, free food, or wellness programs if offered? This shows if the company truly values and encourages their use, or if they're just listed benefits.

- **New Employee Onboarding:** How are new hires integrated? Is there a formal buddy system, or are they expected to figure things out themselves? This reflects the culture of support and mentorship.

- **Language and Jargon:** Pay attention to company-specific acronyms, jargon, or inside jokes. This can reveal the internal "tribe" and how quickly newcomers are expected to adapt.

Engage and Participate

You can't truly understand and shape workplace culture without engaging in it. The immersion process is necessary; anything less could result in siloing and being kept out of the loop, which is terrible in an executive role. You probably already know this, but make the time to attend company-wide meetings not just as a spectator but also as an active participant. Join social events— even those outside your comfort zone—to build genuine connections.

Seek out engineers, product managers, and marketers; schedule informal coffee chats, join their stand-ups, and understand their challenges. If your company hosts a hackathon, don't just send your team; participate yourself, collaborate with developers, and demonstrate the power of design thinking. Don't observe the culture; contribute to it. By actively engaging, you become a vital part of the company's fabric.

Understand Core Values and Practices

Learn and understand the core values that drive the company. Study the mission and vision statements and observe how well the values they espouse show up in the day-to-day. If "user-centricity" is a core value, note how much user research informs product development and how much user feedback is incorporated into design iterations.

If you sense a misalignment with the organization's values and your own, it suggests you're ready to transition to the next stage of your career. With this awareness, it's wise to take action before the company takes notice; otherwise, it could lead to messages from recruiters, disappointing performance reviews, and making the work you loved something you now dread.

If you cannot leave to pursue another role, get a coach or mentor who can help you reframe the emotional impact of your work to be manageable. Setting a time frame for how long you will stay is part of this process, as is creating a plan for what you really want to do with your life. If you have wanted to be someone or do something but you haven't been able to achieve it on your own, a coach will help you identify what's holding you back, co-create a roadmap for where you want to go, and support you in getting there.

PRIORITIZE YOUR WELL-BEING

Focus on Delegation

It wasn't until I traveled internationally to build UX design teams in various countries that I finally understood that continuing to create hands-on product design specifications didn't benefit anyone. I don't know if stopping work on product design specifications felt like slacking off, or if I just didn't truly trust my team to handle the job (I'm so sorry!). After a year of designing and building teams in three countries, working seven days a week across extreme time zone differences—getting me up at 6 am and leaving me still on calls at 10 pm—was taking its toll. As much as I loved everything I was doing, my mind and body told me this was not sustainable. I was optimizing my life to serve the business while limiting my engagement with the rest of my life. I was on the edge of burnout, but so what? This is life in the tech fast lane. Still, for the sake of the team that was becoming established, I eventually stopped contributing design work and began delegating. You could hear my team sigh with relief! It didn't happen all at once; it took time and a lot of help and support from my team and my coach. Thank you!

Lead with Influence—a Mindset Shift

This shift from hands-on to hands-off leadership signifies a necessary change in mindset. I felt empowered to become an executive, despite feeling anxious about taking on so many new responsibilities. These new tasks included attending board meetings, building teams in international locations, participating in executive off-sites, transforming business objectives into design goals, and delivering quarterly highlights of the team's work and contributions to the business. They required me to enhance my communication with people I didn't know, maintain a positive intent, and be proactive in reaching out to build connections with individuals who were unfamiliar with me. It also meant repeating myself more than I preferred because, as a former boss advised, the seventh time you hear yourself saying something may be the first time someone else hears it.

Feel the Fear and Do It Anyway

In the top job, you will face challenges beyond your comfort zone that naturally evoke fear. Every fiber of your being tells you that some version of this is impossible. What if I fail? I can't do this; it's impossible, ridiculous, crazy, and frightening. But the truth is, you wouldn't be asked to take on something insurmountable if the folks handing out this task didn't think you could give it a go.

Ask Yourself

- What is the shortest distance to finding an answer?

- What is the best use of my time?

Another way of turning emotions into solutions is Byron Katie's *The Work*,[7] which involves asking yourself core questions, they are:

- Is it true?

- Can I absolutely know that it's true?

---

[7] "Byron Katie." *Wikipedia*. April 8, 2006. Accessed June 10, 2025. https://en.wikipedia.org/wiki/Byron_Katie

- How do I react, what happens, when I believe that thought?

- Who would I be without the thought?

Tip: If you're grappling with a dilemma, consider inputting it into an AI platform and applying Byron Katie's "The Work" formula, including the "turnaround" process. While this approach might not allow for the same depth of emotional processing as working through it yourself, it can provide answers much more quickly. Crucially, it offers a fresh perspective you might not reach while agonizing over challenging situations. This can be invaluable for conundrums like "Layoffs are coming, what do I do?" or "My new boss is a bully, what do I do?"—you get the idea.

I didn't always have the skill or resources above to know how to deal with new situations at work. Instead, I would waste hours ruminating and wallowing in confusion. For example, when I was made senior design director at Yahoo, I was invited to join a daily call with sales, business development, marketing, and engineering executives I had not worked with before. This was my first opportunity to be included in an executive conversation. I struggled to keep up with their business banter.

I wanted to provide a concise update on my team's progress toward the business unit's objectives. Although familiar with the metrics discussed, I lacked the perspective to align my team's work with those goals daily. Our work spanned across products and services for PCs, mobile phones, and TVs that would enable Yahoo users to access their personalized content and information from any device. I felt like an impostor for not knowing how to prioritize the details of our project in business terms. I could share updates on our human-centered, qualitative, and iterative design progress. However, what constituted hard metrics was elusive, made me defensive, and I felt out of place and like an impostor every morning.

A former Apple boss once told me he felt like an impostor whenever he updated Steve Jobs (former CEO of Apple): "You say too little, he thinks you're stupid. You say too much; he thinks you're stupid." I now understand what he meant. Sure, I attended this high-level meeting, surrounded by some of the brightest minds in tech—but who was I? Did I truly deserve my place at the table? Did my talent justify my presence?

Every morning, I was unhappy, agitated, and off my game. I lacked the tools to manage my emotions and detach from the stress, so I felt like an impostor for feeling miserable during the day. The misery got to me, so I made unhealthy food choices, gained weight, and felt lonely. I was scared to ask for help, thinking that would be a sure sign to my team that I was failing them. I didn't know how to disengage, so I carried that stress like a heavy bag.

> *"Confidence means believing in yourself. If you don't*
> *believe that what you have to offer is of any value,*
> *well, no one's going to pay for it."*
> *David Airey*

According to Ann Betz in her podcast, The Neuroscience of Resilient Leadership, my system's chemicals to cope with my stress-inducing daily stand-up calls were overstimulating, releasing too much dopamine and norepinephrine into my prefrontal cortex. Because I was not able to de-stress and allow these chemicals to release me from their grip, they contributed to my impaired functioning and poor decision-making. If I'd let this continue, I could have reduced my empathy and led to black-and-white thinking

Today, many large companies recognize impostor syndrome as a barrier to productivity and offer education and training. If you feel overwhelmed by impostor syndrome, consider Valerie Young's insights in her book *The Secret Thoughts of Successful Women.*[8] She states, "Your script is the automatic mental tape that begins playing in situations that trigger your impostor feelings." When embarking on a new job or project, instead of thinking, "Wait until they find out I have no idea what I'm doing," try to think, "Everyone who starts something new feels off-balance at first. I may not have all the answers, but I'm smart enough to find them."

Her book taught me how to reframe my feelings, shift my perspective, evaluate the situation, and free myself from impostor syndrome. Her reframing tools help me de-stress my brain. Here are some examples.

It's OK to Feel Like a Fraud

I had every right to doubt myself and feel like a fraud. As one of the first women in my field to break through this particular glass ceiling and be on the daily standup, it was natural for me to feel uneasy during this call. So why did I see my self-doubt as a sign of my shortcomings instead of a typical reaction to being an outsider? Duh!

---

[8] Young, Valerie. "10 Steps You Can Use to Overcome Impostor Syndrome." November 28, 2017. Accessed April 25, 2025. https://impostorsyndrome.com/articles/10-steps-overcome-impostor/

Separate Feelings From Facts

I wish someone had pointed out my lack of perspective on this situation and helped me separate my intensely conflicted and negative feelings from the facts. I felt stupid for not knowing what to say, but did that mean I was stupid? No!

Break Your Silence

I felt isolated and, shamefully, hid my feelings of inadequacy during those calls. My greatest regret is not breaking that silence and confiding in my supporters. After five fulfilling years with the company, I hit a wall when attempting to climb the corporate ladder; the skills that had served me well simply weren't sufficient for the challenges ahead. It was then that HR recommended an executive coach to help me grow as a leader and improve my communication with business leaders. What I discovered was eye-opening: the business leaders on the calls actually wanted my input, and it was my own attitude and delivery that prevented me from being understood! I was clearly sabotaging myself by allowing my emotions to take over. I had constructed a false narrative, a hypnotic frenzy of fear about not possessing every business detail, when in reality, my participation wasn't limited to just that.

Revise Self-Imposed Rules

As a first-time senior director for a public company, I felt like I needed to have all the answers and never ask for help. I didn't want to appear weak in others' eyes. Who set these rules? In coaching training, I discovered that the "rules" we hold in our minds are intended to keep us safe but can actually hinder our growth. The most common and universal rule maker or saboteur is "The Judge," which affects everyone. It relentlessly criticizes you for mistakes or shortcomings, obsessively warns you about potential risks, keeps you awake at night with worry, and fixates on what is wrong in your life or with others.

My judge saboteur wanted to protect me from appearing weak, so instead of seeking help, I internalized the stress of feeling like an impostor. This left me unhappy, withdrawn, and isolated. I spent many sessions with Ed, my coach, simply discussing what had happened to me during those calls. I began to realize how powerful the judge was in contributing to the traumatic situation I was creating for myself each day. Over time, this began to affect me.

In his book, *Positive Intelligence*, Shirzad Chamine explains that the key to mental fitness is weakening our internal saboteurs, particularly the judge, whose negativity hinders our ability to respond effectively to challenges.[9] Uncovering the layers of rules, processes, practices, and beliefs that no longer serve us is fascinating and inspiring, and it is a rewarding experience to witness. This work served as a precursor to triggering a transformation in my life.

The transformation within me, ignited by having a coach, helped me cultivate self-appreciation, look beyond my current limiting beliefs, and envision a brighter future that aligned more closely with who I am becoming.

Ask for Help

Working with my coach provided tools to recognize and loosen the grip that my judge had on my life. Without this change, I wouldn't have been able to establish a new 'script.' Today, I interact

---

[9] "Positive Intelligence | Building mental fitness for all." *Positive Intelligence*. Accessed April 25, 2025. https://www.positiveintelligence.com/

with the business leaders on the call in ways I didn't before. I strive to understand what they enjoy about their jobs, what makes them anxious, and how they define success. I inquired about their experiences with design teams, expectations, preferred collaboration style, and what an effective update from me would look like. Trust me when I say overcoming self-doubt is essential for significantly impacting one's life and leadership.

Trust the People Who Trust You

Phil Clevenger, in his interview in Chapter One, talks about how when impostor syndrome kicks in, he feels insecure, out of his league, or unwelcome by new executive peers. But he has a secret trick to dealing with it that I want to remind us of: "I recall all the insanely smart and talented people who have believed in me and put me in the roles I have had. Surely, those people cannot have been wrong time and time again! This helpful silent exercise can calm even the most acute episode."

Set boundaries: Protect Your Time and Energy

In leadership, you will find that meetings can take up a lot of time. This can be exhausting if you thrive in solitude like I do. My social energy has its limits, and what became non-negotiable for me as a leader was having control over part of my day. This meant getting up very early to do my physical workouts, engage in mental meditation and spiritual prayers, and mentally rehearse the day ahead, envisioning all the problems solved, solutions provided, and positive outcomes. What works for me may not work for you; however, trust me when I say that every executive I've ever met has a set of established disciplines they practice to keep the wheels on their luxury badass bus rolling in top gear.

To supercharge your morning routine, consider the insights of Dr. Benjamin Hardy,[10] an organizational psychologist and author. He offers a wealth of free resources designed to help you strengthen your boundaries, protect your valuable time, and empower you to be at your best more often. I also find the Brendon Burchard Performance Planner and journal invaluable for strategic thinking, effective daily prioritization, and maintaining a positive mindset.[11]

If I were to recommend just one addition to your morning routine to help protect your time and energy, it would be Morning Pages. Introduced by Julia Cameron in *The Artist's Way*,[12] this practice involves three pages of long-hand, stream-of-consciousness writing done first thing in the morning. Its primary goal is to clear your mind of clutter and free up creative energy by getting thoughts, feelings, and worries out of your head and onto the page.

The gist of all this is simple: establish routines for parts of your day that allow you to include time for all aspects of your life. Because, in case you forgot (as I have in the past), there are really only four things that truly matter: dreams, relationships, wealth, and health.

---

[10] Be Your Future Self Now: The Science of Intentional Transformation Paperback – August 1, 2023 by Dr. Benjamin Hardy

[11] The High Performance Planner Diary – Day to Day Calendar, November 2, 2018 by Brendon Burchard

[12] The Artist's Way: 30th Anniversary Edition Paperback – October 25, 2016 by Julia Cameron

Build a Support System

The work is challenging, the problems complex, so having a support system to help you gather diverse perspectives, receive practical assistance, feel connected to others, and reduce stress levels is non-negotiable. You have the support of your team and special people you trust at work, but what about support outside of work? Who will you confide in regarding what you can't discuss at work? Where can you find emotional support and help achieve a sense of balance? Who could help relieve some of the pressure?

Leadership is a lonely pursuit, so if you intend to keep this top-level position, please build a support system as a safety net to navigate life's challenges effectively. Feeling connected to others can help reduce feelings of loneliness and isolation.

TAKE ACTION WHEN THINGS GO WRONG

It's easy to let recruiters and friends guide our career paths, sometimes leading us astray until we suddenly find ourselves struggling. But it doesn't have to be this way. To ensure you're always steering your own ship, let's look at why even top executive leaders can stumble.

If your professional journey isn't going as planned, it often boils down to one of four common reasons: you stayed in a role too long; you accepted an offer that was too good to refuse (even if it wasn't the right fit); you settled for whatever job was available; or your company was acquired, changing everything. Somewhere along the way, you might have lost sight of your true purpose—or perhaps your purpose evolved as your leadership influence grew. Let's dive into these four potential traps and explore how you can get your career back on track.

You Stayed Too Long

Transitioning to a new company can be significantly more complicated for someone deeply entrenched in their previous role for an extended period. Imagine spending a decade at the forefront of user experience design for top financial technology (fintech) companies, only to accept a prestigious leadership position at a major financial institution. Culture shock may become an issue; here's why.

Moving from a fast-paced, innovative tech environment to a more traditional, hierarchical organization like a bank is a far bigger change than most people might expect. Tech leaders who are used to questioning everything might find the slower pace, top-down management, and siloed work frustrating. Adapting to this new environment means navigating rigid hierarchies, making decisions despite uncertainty, and proactively reaching out to people even when it's not explicitly required.

When you change roles after a long tenure, an initial lack of experience and a limited network of supporters can impede your ability to communicate confidently and keep pace effectively. At your new company, you'll need to invest significant time and effort into establishing new connections and earning the trust of your colleagues. This involves quickly grasping complex power dynamics and informal networks to influence decisions and achieve your goals.

Resistance to change, often a byproduct of a long tenure, can hinder your ability to adapt to new environments and accept new challenges. While adopting a growth mindset will help you overcome this aversion, it's best to reduce the risks of culture shock before you even switch companies by asking yourself:

- Am I inspired by the work and the people enough to truly invest in learning about them and the culture?

- This will be a big adjustment; am I well and fit enough to take on this challenge?

- Where am I becoming complacent or resistant to change simply because I'm moving from an established role where I'm known, respected, and supported?

They Made You an Offer You Could Not Refuse

If you accept a job mainly for a compelling long-term financial offer, you may find it challenging to thrive for several reasons. First, your motivations might not align. When financial gain is your primary driver (extrinsic motivation), it can overshadow motivators like passion for the work, belief in the company's mission, or a desire for professional growth (intrinsic motivation). This lack of intrinsic motivation can result in lower engagement, reduced effort, and poorer performance. Second, concentrating on long-term financial incentives, such as stock options that vest years down the line, can distract you from the immediate demands of the job. This distraction may hinder your ability to focus on learning, building relationships, and contributing effectively in the early stages, which are critical for long-term success.

If you aren't genuinely invested in the company's mission or culture you may put less effort into understanding the nuances of how things operate there. A lack of cultural integration can hinder your ability to collaborate effectively and navigate the organizational landscape.

When a company invests in hiring you, it's natural for high expectations to arise. You may feel pressured to demonstrate your value quickly. If your skills or experience don't perfectly align with the role's demands, you may find it challenging to meet these expectations, resulting in stress and potential underperformance. The pressure to "prove your worth" can become a significant burden, hindering your ability to contribute meaningfully over the long term. At the same time, you concentrate on achieving short-term wins to justify the investment made in you.

Sometimes, even with the best intentions, your priorities and the market can shift, changing the landscape of your work. Additionally, changes in your circumstances may make the initial financial incentive feel less significant than it once did. A major life event, like a health scare, bereavement, menopause, or pregnancy, could prompt you to reassess what you want from your career and redirect your focus away from work. Market fluctuations can influence the value of items like stock options or other long-term incentives. If those values decline significantly, you might feel demotivated or resentful, which will likely affect your performance if it's the main reason you took the job.

If financial gain is your sole focus, you may neglect your professional development or miss out on growth opportunities within the company, which could lead to career stagnation and a lack of fulfillment. If you prioritize monetary gain over essential factors like cultural fit, intrinsic motivation, and professional growth, you will likely face challenges at a new tech company, even with an attractive compensation package.

Ask Yourself

- Beyond the money and perks, does this role truly excite me and align with my long-term career aspirations?

- Does this company feel like a place where I'll build genuine social connections and find mentors, ensuring it's more than just a transactional relationship?

- Am I genuinely excited about the future of this merged entity, or am I holding onto the past of my previous company?

Your Company Gets Acquired

Conversely, you might encounter a significant culture clash when your company is acquired. The changes in your role and responsibilities, reporting structure, along with the redundancies accompanying an acquisition, may create uncertainty and anxiety about your job security. The acquiring company's strategic priorities and product roadmaps might differ significantly from what you're used to. You may find yourself involved in projects you are less passionate about, or do not fully utilize your skills.

When companies merge, significant integration challenges often arise. Merging different systems, processes, and technologies can be complicated. This may result in inefficiencies, confusion, and frustration as you adjust to new working methods.

Leadership and talented employees from the acquired company often leave. The departure of experienced individuals can create a void within your new team, potentially impacting its overall performance and complicating your transition.

Feeling undervalued or misunderstood if the acquiring company does not fully leverage your expertise or acknowledge the value you brought from the acquired organization is discouraging. This issue can worsen due to an "us vs. them" mentality that may develop between employees of both organizations, fostering division and hindering collaboration, ultimately leaving you feeling isolated and unappreciated.

Ask Yourself

- Will I have the autonomy and resources needed to drive meaningful change and innovation? Or will I be constantly fighting against new bureaucratic hurdles?

- Are the people I admire and want to work with still present, or have key individuals already departed?

- Does this acquisition ultimately benefit my long-term career goals and align with my values as a design leader?

You Were Desperate and Took What Was Offered

Desperation can lead to accepting a job without fully understanding the role, company culture, or expectations. This mismatch can result in disappointment, frustration, and feeling unprepared. Desperation can weaken your negotiating position, causing you to accept lower salaries, fewer benefits, or less favorable terms. This may breed resentment and dissatisfaction toward others.

Individuals who feel desperate may focus so intensely on keeping their job that they have difficulty adapting, leading to challenges in integrating at the company. You might feel pressure to quickly prove your value, resulting in anxiety and haste in completing tasks, which can lead to mistakes and lower-quality work. This can create a negative feedback loop that further impacts your confidence.

The combination of stress, pressure, and misaligned motivation can heighten the risk of burnout, leading to decreased productivity, absenteeism, and ultimately, job dissatisfaction or even resignation. Sometimes, desperation may cause you to exaggerate your skills or experience during the interview process. This can quickly become apparent in the workplace, resulting in performance issues.

Ask Yourself

- Beyond the paycheck, what truly excites or frustrates me about this specific role on a day-to-day basis? (This helps separate the financial motivation from the actual work.)

- What is the precise financial threshold I need to meet to feel secure and comfortable, and does this role exceed that by so much that it justifies the other frustrations? (Pinpointing your actual financial need versus perceived opportunity.)

- Have I thoroughly researched the company's culture, values, and leadership?

- If I left this job, how long could I comfortably sustain myself while looking for a better fit? (Assessing your financial runway.)

Mastering Executive Leadership: Beyond the Title

So, as you can see, thriving as a tech executive design leader is about much more than just landing the top job. It's an ongoing journey that demands you constantly prove your value, build strong alliances, and stay at the forefront of innovation. You'll need to communicate with exceptional clarity, ask incisive questions, meticulously build your personal brand, and wholeheartedly embrace change with remarkable resilience.

On top of all that, truly flourishing means deeply understanding your company's culture, vigilantly prioritizing your own well-being, and having the courage to take decisive action when challenges arise. These aren't just good ideas; they're non-negotiable for not just surviving, but truly flourishing at the pinnacle of your career.

To bring all these principles to life and gain even deeper insights into the realities of sustained executive design leadership, let's hear from someone who embodies them.

Colin Grigson is the Design Director at Remitly, a company revolutionizing international money transfers. He leads a team dedicated to optimizing the user experience for millions of customers across 170 countries. His rich background includes leading product design teams at diverse tech giants like RingCentral, Redfin, Apptio, and Expedia, with formative design roles at PayPal, Doxo, Amazon, and Dell. Colin's journey offers a unique lens into the strategies and mindset required not only to secure, but critically, to keep the top job in design.

EXECUTIVE INSIGHT WITH COLIN GRIGSON

What did your journey to executive leadership look like?

My leadership journey started early. As a teenager, I worked in a grocery store and became one of the youngest managers at 19. As a store manager, the people I managed were either much older than me or much younger in high school. I was a kid, you know, telling them what to do. These high school kids couldn't care less that they were there.

I learned to adopt a soft leadership style focused on helping people feel supported and fostering relationships. I occasionally took a stand when things seemed to veer off track, and they allowed me to be decisive because of the rapport I had built with them.

This experience was an early lesson in leadership without formal authority. I had to learn how to influence people through relationships by understanding their needs. I was motivating them based on their desires and goals without even realizing it. Looking back, I gained valuable survival skills in that role, which have laid a solid foundation for my leadership style.

So, I naturally gravitated toward management roles. After working at the grocery store, I transitioned to our gallery coffee shop, which allowed me to pursue my design passions. I was responsible for all their design work, and it was a fantastic way to immerse myself in an artistic community.

Growing up in a small Texas town, I was surrounded by people who encouraged my unconventional interests.

While my high school offered welding and auto mechanics classes, I was captivated by computer graphics and web design. Being among like-minded individuals who supported my aspirations was truly inspiring.

> *"I had to learn how to influence people through relationships by understanding their needs."*

I began as a barista and quickly advanced to a management role. After a year, I recognized that I was reverting to familiar patterns. A similar path unfolded in the tech industry, where I naturally assumed supportive roles and reached my objectives.

I've always cared about the 'why.' I always wondered, "Why do we do things this way?" even when I worked at the grocery store. I always cared about this. That, combined with the gratification I get from supporting people, helping them be happy, and accomplishing their goals, is probably at the core of my identity as a leader.

What led you to move from retail to the tech industry?

Yeah, it was an interesting time. I was about 21, unsure about my future, and drifting in and out of community college. But then, something shifted. I remembered my passion for computers, digital art, and web design. I'd been teaching myself coding and Photoshop for years.

So, I began diving back in. I took on projects such as designing websites and marketing materials for local businesses. I even contributed to a small magazine, crafting those cringey little ads for antique shops. It was quite a humbling experience, but I learned a lot and sharpened my skills.

It's like all these little things. I could've spent $25 on a small ad or something, but I was thrilled to create something that went out into the world. It was incredibly satisfying. Then, I started building websites for local businesses, which was really fun. I decided, "I want to do design. This is what I love and care about deeply."

Once I made that decision, things started to fall into place. I planned to move to Austin for six months and apply to the University of Texas's design program. One of our regulars asked me to design a website for her, and I thought, "Yeah, I'd love to do that!"

She knew someone who owned a company and offered to contact him on my behalf. I was surprised but grateful for her initiative. She helped me polish my resume and cover letter, and soon enough, I was interviewing and landing a job. It was a whirlwind experience, and I dropped out of college to pursue this opportunity in Austin, working for a small agency as a website designer.

Back in the brochure days, websites had the standard "About Services" section, which was a pretty typical experience. But this was different. It was a really good experience for me. It allowed me to ease into the industry, and I had some great mentors along the way.

It wasn't a clean break, but it let me dive in and learn in a way that suited me. As an adult, I realized I have ADHD, and now that I understand it better, it's amazing how different learning and motivation styles can be. That's been a real privilege for me lately. Understanding how people's brains work is a longer conversation, but I think understanding it has made me a better leader.

So, that's how it happened. That's how I transitioned to tech full-time. Eventually, this experience built my portfolio, which helped me secure a contract position with Dell, which later turned into a full-time job. This opportunity opened the door to Amazon.

Once again, it revolves around decision-making. One of my managers contemplated leaving Texas to relocate to the West Coast. He had a contact at Amazon and brought it up to me. Sometimes, you simply make a choice, and if people care about you, they'll be eager to support you and help you find happiness.

I've made an effort to support those around me—my friends, family, and team. I believe we should prioritize people over employees. It's easy to forget, especially as managers, that our role isn't just to represent and protect the company but also to care for the designers and team members. As we've seen in recent years, companies ultimately need to do what's best for themselves. It's a business, and I understand that. However, we, the people, are the true community. That's how I strive to prioritize my loyalties.

What's your leadership vision for design at Remitly?

Initially, I wasn't overly concerned with the specific job title or the rigid responsibilities of the role. What truly drew me to the position was the people, the company culture, and the mission. As I've matured in my career, I've realized that these intangible factors are the real drivers of long-term motivation and passion. Unlike job titles or specific responsibilities, these elements are more enduring and can evolve as the company grows and changes.

I started on the design systems team and contributed to the user experience of the performance app. I lead all product designers for the core events app and the design system. Most of the product designers now report to me.

The design team is growing rapidly, tripling in size in just a couple of years. We're at a crucial juncture where we must take the next big leap. One of my primary goals for next year is to establish a culture of design excellence. I'm working on a strategy focusing on a number of key areas:

Change Our Mindset

Within the team and the company, we need to consider how we might change our processes. Remitly's product development process has a very 'limitations first' mindset. We start by defining what engineering can publish and then work backward. While this is one approach to building things, it's not necessarily the best way, right?

> *"To celebrate greatness and inspire others to reach their full potential, we need to foster a healthy and supportive environment."*

Focus on Customer-Centricity

We start by identifying the customer's pain points and their business challenges. Then, we determine the optimal solution and break it down into achievable milestones that deliver value. This requires cultural shifts, such as recognizing and celebrating exceptional work. We have a somewhat 'everyone gets a trophy' culture, which, while fostering appreciation, can obscure truly outstanding contributions. By highlighting exceptional work, the team can learn and grow from the best examples.

To celebrate greatness and inspire others to reach their full potential, we need to foster a healthy and supportive environment. This involves creating a supportive environment where individuals can focus on their strengths and contribute to the team's overall success. It means avoiding a competitive culture and instead focusing on inspiration and growth. By surrounding ourselves with talented and humble individuals, we can create a space where people feel empowered to learn and develop their skills.

Celebrate Diverse Perspectives

Another crucial aspect of this framework is highlighting diverse skill sets. We can foster a more inclusive and innovative culture by showcasing different talents and perspectives.

Conduct Effective Performance Management

We're investing in writing explicit career ladders and performance management expectations. By providing clear pathways for growth and regular feedback, we can help our team members achieve their goals. By combining these approaches, we can create a workplace that celebrates excellence and supports our team members' growth and development. This empowers managers to directly address performance issues, clearly communicate expectations, and provide opportunities for improvement. If necessary, it equips managers with the tools to swiftly manage underperforming individuals, making room for high-potential talent with the right attitude and cultural fit.

Encourage People Skills

While there are incentives to motivate positive performance, it's crucial to remember that developing people skills is a key component of effective management. I'm excited about a more strategic, purposeful approach to team learning. Imagine a "storytelling quarter" where we all commit to mastering storytelling. We can celebrate our team's natural storytellers, who can lead workshops, share resources, or invite guest speakers. We'll allocate about 10% of everyone's time to design excellence to make this happen. This means scheduling dedicated time for learning and skill-sharing. By empowering and equipping our team, we can level up collectively. I believe this experiment will foster a more open and vulnerable team culture. When we focus on the team's growth, individuals feel less pressure and are more willing to learn and share.

Create Shared Goals

We are exploring this area, which I think could be really powerful and give the team a common goal. As leaders, we can strategically choose areas to focus on. For instance, our team could delve into storytelling or service design.

Service design is particularly relevant for remote teams and an area I'm eager to learn more about. Once we cover the core curriculum, we can introduce more specialized topics like analytics or business acumen. This allows us to build on the team's foundational skills and address specific needs.

Deliver Quality Design

This is where I think design teams sometimes get into trouble. They try to skip a step. They try to start caring about business analytics and getting involved too early. Then, they're not doing their core job very well. I'm always a fan of earning the right to sit at the table by doing our job well. That's the value we bring. Do that well, and you earn permission to start getting your hands dirty with the other stuff. But if you're not delivering your core work, you're not adding much value. You're just another person in the room.

Give Designers the Right Tools

I don't think asking people to do great work without giving them great tools is fair. Is our design system up to snuff? Do we have the right tools in place? How are people doing prototyping? Are they being appropriately supported? It's all in service of the team. Are we doing everything we can?

It's a lot like our design platform team, right? They're there to support design systems and the overall design process. What I like about this framework, which provides guidelines and support, is its evergreen nature. We can tackle different topics within each bucket, quarter, or year. For example, revamping our career ladders made progress in one bucket. In addition, we're working on a new product development model with the product officer to streamline our approach.

Improve Execution Capabilities

My goal for next year is to help the team improve their execution capabilities. It's a big undertaking, but I'm excited about the potential. I enjoy this kind of work because it aligns with what many colleagues appreciate. I love getting the team excited and motivated. I want to transform remote work into a space where investing in the right tools and design can lead to exceptional work.

Empower Proactive Transformation

Too often, people wait for change to happen to them. Instead, we should actively participate in shaping our work environment. We need a framework to guide this transformation. My job is to help motivate, inspire, and empower them. I provide the framework they need to contribute, but then I step back and let them drive the culture change with us.

As a design leader, I believe in empowering people with the tools to think critically rather than providing a rigid instruction manual. Processes can often become overly prescriptive, which can be counterproductive in the dynamic world of design. Every project is unique, and a one-size-fits-all approach rarely yields optimal results. Instead, I focus on providing people with the tools to quickly assess a situation and determine the best approach. Frameworks are instrumental in this regard.

Build Design and System Frameworks

They offer a structured way to break down complex problems into simpler components. For example, when discussing a complex concept, a framework can help distill it into two key points that can be easily explained in an elevator pitch. I've applied this approach to the question of driving excellence. By categorizing the key factors into three distinct buckets, I've created a simple yet powerful framework that guides our team toward achieving our goals. Within that framework, we can now define workstreams and specific actions. I'm a strong pattern recognizer, so I'm naturally drawn to finding order in chaos. I excel at creating frameworks that help everyone understand complex situations. When I think of frameworks, I envision a mental construct that provides structure and clarity.

What's your perspective on the "done is better than perfect"?

I'm way more pragmatic than I used to be. Early in my career, it was more about the need to be perfect. However, too often, "move fast and break things" is the default. I am encouraging our product partners to adopt a more strategic mindset. Too often, it feels like we need to test and learn. I'm like, "No, we need to learn and learn." Spending some time upfront is okay to ensure we're testing something impactful. When the team wants to test everything without thinking it through, I'm like, "Guys, that's a waste of resources."

I'm realizing now that I try to take the longer view. I look at it like, "Is this better than before? Is this building us in the right direction?" Nothing will ever be perfect, and I'm uncomfortable with that fact. But it is a fact. We're a collection of humans building something. Imperfection is inevitable.

No design and no engineering solution is perfect. Something's always going to give. We're human, and mistakes happen. It's about accepting that reality. Ultimately, the question is: Are you proud of the work? Are the compromises acceptable? Does the final product satisfy customers and achieve its goals? Are we continually improving?

I've shifted my perspective to focus on progress. Are we moving in the right direction?

And I think that's the right approach versus "done is better than perfect." When that's your mindset, you're brute-forcing things, pushing to get them done quickly, but you're not actually teaching people or helping them grow. This quick fix might seem appealing, but it doesn't lead to lasting change. The longer-term approach, while slower, is more effective. You create a sustainable solution by investing time in developing people's skills and knowledge.

One caveat is figuring out how to balance these two approaches tactically. Not all organizations have the patience for a gradual, long-term strategy. They often look outward and demand immediate results, expecting their design org to be at peak performance immediately. They don't always realize that a high-functioning design organization relies on the strength of other parts of the business. It's a team effort, not a solo act.

Anyway, I'm realizing that there are key strategic moments when design needs to step up and deliver at a really high level. This helps build credibility and secure the investment needed to keep moving forward.

Right now, I'm focused on investing in a few key individuals who are starting to show real potential. Instead of forcing them into a specific mold, I want to empower and support them to create examples of excellence. I want to guide them, but still let the team do the work. I'm trying to balance pushing for excellence, protecting the rest of the team, and helping them grow.

How do you inspire excellence?

Right now, I'm focused on a couple of key strategies. One involves a team member transitioning from a management role to a senior IC position. While incredibly talented and experienced, she's facing challenges adapting to this new role. I'm working to support her by rebalancing the team to free up my time and provide the specific guidance she needs.

The second strategy involves a critical project. I have someone who's technically skilled but heavily burdened with other priorities. I'm looking to reassign this project to another team member with the necessary skills and capacity to deliver it effectively. So, I'm trying to find a hybrid solution to assemble folks who can help deliver and support them as coaches, not hands-on contributors.

How do you ensure your team's work contributes to the company's bottom line?

Early in my career, I focused solely on doing what was right for the user. Unfortunately, designers often get caught up in fixing problems without considering the long-term business impact. Sure, we could build all sorts of features that users would love, but do they align with our strategic goals?

For example, imagine we're building a peer-to-peer payment app. Users might request a debit card for in-store purchases, but it's not the right move if that would negatively impact our business model. We also see trends like contactless payments suggesting debit cards might decline.

There's often tension between what customers say they want and what we see as their actual needs. Then, there's the balancing act of maintaining a healthy business while anticipating future needs. Considering all these factors, I'm learning to take a more holistic view.

I've always been wary of separating 'business goals' from 'user goals.' In a healthy organization, these should intertwine. When people split them, it can pit design against the business, creating artificial tension. It's like saying, "We have our truth; you have yours."

So, rather than insisting on our individual viewpoints, we'll aim to find a shared perspective that benefits both our customers and our business. We'll encourage everyone to ground their ideas in hypotheses and consider the broader implications for the business. We'll strive for a unified approach instead of a "this or that" mentality.

How do we bridge the gap when designers and engineers disagree on technical limitations?

It's funny; it's not necessarily the engineers' skills. It's more about the culture we've created. We've built a fast-paced environment, and engineers often respond by taking the easy route. I don't doubt that they'd love to spend more time and build things better, but that's not always the priority.

I don't believe it's scalable to constantly expect designers to push engineering teams for perfection. This approach might work in a startup, but we need to consider how everything scales in larger organizations. And so, the tools and components engineers use to build products should be reusable. A button, for example, shouldn't be fixed on a single product. Instead, it should be improved in the shared component library used across the entire product suite.

We must invest heavily in design systems and components to achieve this scale and quality in UI and engineering. This allows us to perfect each element once and reuse it throughout the product, maximizing efficiency and ensuring consistency. Teams should collaborate closely with design systems experts to foster this systems-thinking mindset. The focus should shift from what's best for an individual area to what's best for the entire app, team, and company.

Our company is in an emerging growth phase, maturing into a mindset where we're looking at the broader ecosystem and scaling. People used to focus on personal experiences and what worked for them. There's a shift towards doing what's right for the whole system. It's an interesting combination of a systems mindset and a focus on individual experiences. I think that's how we achieve truly great outcomes.

It's a trade-off between short-term fixes and long-term solutions. While you can easily override specific issues and achieve quick wins, that doesn't address the underlying systemic problems.

I focus on building a strong foundation through design systems and component libraries. This takes time but is the key to long-term, sustainable improvement. It's about striking a balance between immediate needs and strategic goals. Sometimes, you must fight the good fight, even when the quick fix is tempting.

How do you prioritize impactful design with limited resources?

I guess I don't see it as my decision. It's usually something I work closely on with the product team. Recently, we faced resource constraints, with some areas being more limited than others. This led to tough trade-off conversations.

The key is getting product partners to value design. We must shift their mindset from "if design can't do it, we'll figure it out" to "if design can't do it, it can't be done." This creates the necessary urgency within the organization to secure the funding and resources for design support. Ultimately, product and design partners must be aligned on the importance of design in delivering high-quality products.

I can shout from the rooftops about needing more resources, but I'll likely be ignored. Everyone's busy building their little empires, right? Whether that's their intention or not, it's the reality. Leaders hear these complaints constantly, especially from people who don't have a direct stake in the budget.

However, it catches their attention when product and engineering teams start echoing these concerns. That's when they realize it's a real problem that needs addressing. Building relationships and trust is key. I have a great relationship with our product partners. We met yesterday to discuss next year's priorities and how we'll support them. Here's something I said to one of our product partners:

"I want to make sure he's aligned with our goals. Here's the message I need your help with: We're not set up to handle X, Y, Z. If we were, I'd need your support in areas where I can't be, helping to communicate the message. That's the only way to build support. You don't succeed if I don't succeed, right?"

I don't think it's my job to dictate the company's priorities. But it is my job to negotiate with our partners and balance limited resources to focus on the most impactful areas. I trust my product partners. If the business strategy team says expanding into a new country is our biggest opportunity, I trust them. I don't want them second-guessing my resource allocation.

Sure, there are times to argue and debate, but ultimately, we must align with the company's overall strategy.

How do you build trust and collaboration with cross-functional teams, especially when priorities or perspectives clash?

I think it's important to strike a balance between formality and informality. If you're always formal, it can feel distant and impersonal. You want people to see you as a person, not just a coworker.

To do that, you must be willing to be vulnerable and share your experiences. It can be a delicate balance, especially when you're representing a team and fighting for their interests. Sometimes, empathizing too much can feel like a breach of trust.

But I've realized that being open and honest is the best approach. I'm not going to play politics or games. I will be upfront about what's happening and how we can work together. I believe people appreciate authenticity. Whether they can pinpoint it or not, they can feel when someone's not being genuine. So, I've stopped trying to fake it.

We have three engineering leaders who are, let's just say, not exactly seeing eye-to-eye. We need a design system; everyone agrees, but no one wants to take the lead. It's a classic case of passing the buck. So, I finally had to step in and say, "Look, you all figure it out. I don't care how, just do it." I'm trying to be more direct but with kindness. People respond better to honesty, even if it's a bit meandering.

I try to be genuine. I don't hide my own struggles, whether they're with the game or personally. I think being open encourages others to be more open as well. Then, we can have real, meaningful conversations about what's best for the company.

We're all on the same team and must respect each other. I respect my colleagues and the value they bring. I know I can't do an engineer's job, and I don't need to. My role is to support those who excel in that area. I appreciate that they value my input and ask for my opinion. While they make the final decisions, my job is to support them and provide guidance. I just want the same respect in return. Designers often don't get that. But if I'm willing to give it, I expect it in return.

Sometimes, people might say, "You wouldn't want me to do this, would you?" And I'll say, "Of course not, that's crazy." But I also want them to allow my team to make decisions, even if it means they might fail.

I give you all the ability to make decisions and fail. This often happens in teams where the product manager won't let you try something new. It's like, okay, do we have any research to validate this idea? Are we really convinced it's a good idea? If not, you must have that conversation and let the designers experiment.

It often comes down to who feels responsible. People start to feel ownership over the user experience, but design needs to be at the forefront, standing side-by-side with the PM. When the criticism starts, you take the hits. You don't put the PM in front to present the design work. You present it yourself, take the heat, and show them you're on the front lines with them.

And then they start to give you more leeway because they know they're not the ones who will be held accountable for those decisions. You can support each other and explore the root causes of some of the symptoms. I've seen that the more designers take ownership of their decisions, the more they're trusted to make them.

We should be responsible for the usability of the product experience and the solutions we design. We should stand up for our decisions and take ownership of the good and bad outcomes. If something doesn't work, it's our problem to solve.

Too often, designers hide behind product management. We should be more assertive and vocal about our ideas. As you mentioned, it is crucial to support other functions and build vulnerability. We need to stand behind our work and be willing to learn from our mistakes.

Engineering can be a tricky field. I often start by fostering a strong relationship with my cross-functional peers. Most engineers I've encountered genuinely care about building quality products. They may not always share our aesthetic preferences, but they understand the value of good design and user experience. By consistently delivering high-quality work and demonstrating its impact, we can gain the trust and support of product teams.

When approaching engineers, it's important to consider their perspective. They often prioritize scalability and efficiency. We can foster a more productive and collaborative relationship by framing our discussions regarding how our work can improve their ability to build and maintain systems.

Engineers have different love languages, right? So, how do you show up for them in a way that works for them?

Often, designers come in and start changing patterns, and engineers ask, "Why are we changing this? We do it this way everywhere else!" because they're pulling in components, shared assets, and all that. The designers have to come up with answers to these questions, and the engineers might think they're a bit weak. This creates tension because, eventually, someone has to build it, often ending up in this weird in-between place.

And that's why I think involving engineers early in the review process is crucial. They need to be included from the start. One of the biggest challenges engineers face, which takes time to address, is their dual mindset. On one hand, they're constantly asked to deliver solutions within tight constraints. "How long will this take?" "What are the limitations?" These are the questions they're accustomed to answering. However, it's important to encourage them to think beyond these constraints and explore the possibilities.

But for a lot of design work, you're doing the opposite. You're acknowledging the constraints but not letting them dictate the solution. You're asking, "What's the right thing to do?" Then, the constraints help you make the necessary compromises to achieve that goal.

However, when it comes to technology, we should always be pushing the boundaries and evolving. We shouldn't constantly pull back on constraints. So, the challenge is getting engineers, who often operate within specific constraints, to think more creatively and contribute as "yes and" partners. This shift in mindset can make them invaluable to the process.

When you shift into that creative problem-solving mindset, things happen, right? People start thinking, "We have this limitation, but if we connect it to this other thing, we could do it in half the time." Getting them into that mindset is key and takes time and effort, starting with the product and bringing everyone together to focus on it.

CHAPTER 3

How to Impact Tech Empires

HOW DESIGN FUELS TECH'S CORE: SOFTWARE

A tech company isn't just making software—software is its essence. Think of it as the company's DNA. As a design leader, you wield significant influence over it for two fundamental reasons.

Firstly, software's beauty (and power) lies in its near-zero marginal cost. Once you've built it, replicating and distributing it to millions costs nothing. This inherent scalability is the lifeblood of tech growth, driving the relentless pursuit of solutions that can reach massive audiences without a proportional increase in expense. As a design leader, you're on the front lines of enabling this. By championing and implementing modular and reusable design systems, you directly contribute to this scalability, accelerating development cycles, ensuring consistency across expanding product lines, and ultimately, minimizing costs for future innovations.

Secondly, unlike physical products, software is inherently fluid and iterative. It lives and breathes through continuous updates, patches, and constantly introduces new features. This relentless evolution is crucial for staying ahead in a hyper-competitive landscape, where both established players and nimble newcomers are continually vying for user attention. The pressure to iterate quickly often fosters a culture that prioritizes speed to market over absolute perfection in initial releases. Your role is vital in ensuring that this speed doesn't come at the expense of user experience. By strategically implementing processes for gathering user feedback, conducting regular design audits, and embedding the UXD process into the development lifecycle, you champion continuous improvement. This will ensure that the software gets to market fast, evolves intelligently to meet user needs, and maintains a competitive edge.

So, how is this essential software developed within this dynamic environment? You're probably familiar with the principles, but let's quickly revisit the core tenets that shape tech culture and drive the creation of these vital software products and services. They include agile development, innovation, collaboration, customer centricity, and execution.

Agile Development

Agile emerged from a critical need for a more adaptable, responsive, and human-centric approach to software development, moving away from the rigid, sequential "waterfall" methodologies. It was formally established in February 2001 by a group of seventeen independent software practitioners, frustrated with heavy, documentation-driven processes that often led to late, over-budget, and irrelevant software. They drafted the "Manifesto for Agile Software Development," now widely known as the Agile Manifesto.3 This manifesto articulated four core values and twelve supporting principles, prioritizing individuals and interactions, working software, customer collaboration, and responding to change over rigid processes and tools, extensive documentation, strict contract negotiation, and adherence to a fixed plan. You know this already, but understanding and actively supporting the Agile process is absolutely essential for several critical reasons:

- **Ensuring Design Relevance and Impact:** By integrating your team with Agile, you ensure that design decisions are continuously informed by new learnings and directly influence each iteration of the product, leading to more impactful and usable solutions.

- **Fostering Collaboration and Empathy:** Agile thrives on cross-functional collaboration. For you, this means breaking down barriers between design, engineering, product, and quality assurance. Having your team members being part of daily stand-ups, sprint reviews, and retrospectives allows you to share insights, understand technical constraints, and ensure that the user's voice is present and influential throughout the entire development lifecycle.

- **Managing Design Debt and Technical Feasibility:** Agile's iterative nature allows for early identification of design challenges and technical impediments. As a design leader, you can guide your team to balance aspirational design with practical implementation, making informed trade-offs and ensuring that designs are not only user-centered but also technically feasible and sustainable within the product's development cadence. This proactive approach helps prevent the accumulation of design debt and costly rework.

- **Accelerating Learning and Adaptation**: The "inspect and adapt" principle of Agile means constant feedback loops. As design leader embedded in Agile, you can champion continuous user research and usability testing throughout the development process, not just at the beginning or end. This allows for rapid learning about user behavior and market needs, enabling your design team to quickly pivot or refine their solutions based on real data, accelerating the path to product-market fit.

There isn't just one "Agile process"; rather, there are different frameworks and methodologies that embody the Agile principles. Some of the most common you will have come across include:

- **Scrum**: A highly structured framework with fixed-length iterations (sprints), defined roles (Product Owner, Scrum Master, Development Team), and specific events (e.g., daily stand-ups, sprint reviews).

- **Extreme Programming (XP)**: Emphasizes technical practices like pair programming, test-driven development, and continuous integration, often alongside frequent releases.

- **Scaled Agile Framework (SAFe)**: A comprehensive framework for applying Agile principles across large organizations with multiple teams.

- **Kanban** is a visual project management approach that helps teams visualize work, limit work in progress, and boost workflow efficiency. The term originated in the Toyota Production System in the late 1940s, where physical cards signaled the need for materials or to move work along the production line. I've found Kanban invaluable in open office spaces to visually broadcast your team's work, showing dependencies between people and projects. Having everyone gather around the board to give their updates also helps people get to know each other in a more natural, real-life setting. Updates typically follow a format, this is one I prefer:

  1. What's your current status and progress on your assigned tasks? This clarifies where they are, if they're on track, and helps you understand their current workload. It moves beyond a simple "How's it going?" to get concrete details.

  2. Are you encountering any blockers, challenges, or dependencies that are preventing you from moving forward? This helps spot obstacles early. It prompts people to voice anything that might hinder their

progress, allowing for timely intervention and support.

3. What do you plan to complete by our next check-in or by the end of the day/week? This establishes clear short-term goals and helps them prioritize. It ensures alignment on immediate next steps and provides a benchmark for future progress tracking.

4. How can I or the team best support you to overcome any obstacles or accelerate progress? This fosters a supportive environment and emphasizes teamwork. It shifts the focus from individual accountability to collective problem-solving and offers assistance proactively.

- **Lean Startup**: This agile framework originated from Eric Ries in the early 2000s and has become a cornerstone for many startups and entrepreneurs navigating product development uncertainties. While participating in Women 2.0, an incubator program for aspiring entrepreneurs, I learned about Lean Startup from Eric Ries himself. Lean Startup functions through rapid iteration and validated learning.[13] The focus is on developing a minimum viable product (MVP) early on to collect genuine customer feedback. To begin, you create a foundational version of the product with just enough features to draw in early adopters. You identify the problem you are addressing and the core value you provide. Next, you test it with

---

[13] Blank, Steve. "Why the Lean Start-Up Changes Everything." May 1, 2013. Accessed May 5, 2025. https://hbr.org/2013/05/why-the-lean-start-up-changes-everything

users and prepare to implement changes based on their feedback. The feedback cycles are ongoing. A key aspect of this approach is establishing a build-measure-learn feedback loop. Instead of stubbornly preserving something that isn't working, the build-measure feedback loop can enable the company to pivot when necessary. The decision to pivot should be grounded in data rather than relying on gut feeling. By tracking key metrics such as customer acquisition cost, conversion rates, and user engagement, startups can uncover patterns and trends that signal a need for change. For instance, if a product experiences high engagement but has difficulty converting users into paying customers, it may be time to refine the value proposition or explore alternative monetization strategies. Lean Startup emphasizes the importance of learning to measure your actions as quickly and consistently as possible so you can make adjustments quickly. As Eric said, "open your eyes, learn to steer, and you will learn how to get there without crashing."

Collaboration

Seamless collaboration is the engine of innovation and successful product development. It is the vital link that connects diverse expertise, ensuring that different parts of the organization move in concert toward shared goals. As a new design executive, you will find yourself bridging silos and engaging with functional leaders across engineering, product, and marketing departments. While these collaborations are essential for gathering crucial information and aligning on strategic direction—insights your team needs to build effectively—you must also be keenly aware that not all stakeholders will inherently prioritize your team's bandwidth or design-centric perspectives.

Navigating these dynamics requires a strategic approach: You'll need to balance being a collaborative partner with your responsibility to protect your team's focus and ensure design's value isn't diluted or sidelined by broader organizational objectives. To learn more in-depth best practices for collaborating in tech—with your team, cross-functional partners, and executives, and how to identify and work with the four archetypal relationships—see Chapter 8: Relating to Stakeholders.

Innovation

Innovation fuels tech companies to disrupt markets, attract loyal customers, and secure a sustainable future in a fiercely competitive world. Spotify is a tech company disrupting a market, attracting loyal customers, and securing a sustainable future.[14] Spotify's innovation was not just digital music, but a freemium model that offered a vast catalog of music legally, for free (with ads), alongside a premium subscription for an ad-free, on-demand experience. This directly disrupted the traditional sales model of physical albums and even individual digital downloads from platforms like iTunes.

Spotify attracted a massive base of loyal customers through several key design-led features:

- **Vast Library.** Providing access to millions of songs, a scale unimaginable in the physical music era.

---

[14] Naomi. "Spotify Shares Our Vision To Become the World's Creator Platform — Spotify." June 8, 2022. Accessed June 21, 2025. https://newsroom.spotify.com/2022-06-08/spotify-shares-our-vision-to-become-the-worlds-creator-platform/

- **Personalization.** Features like "Discover Weekly," "Release Radar," and "Spotify Wrapped" use sophisticated algorithms to deeply understand user tastes and recommend new music they're likely to love. This created a highly personalized and engaging experience that felt unique to each user.

- **Convenience.** On-demand streaming across multiple devices (phones, computers, smart speakers, cars) made music accessible anywhere, anytime, without the need for downloads or ownership.

- **Social Sharing.** Integrations with social media allowed users to share music and playlists, fostering a sense of community and driving organic discovery.

To secure a sustainable future, Spotify has continually innovated beyond just music streaming. They strategically expanded into podcasting, investing heavily in exclusive content and acquiring companies like Gimlet Media and Anchor.[15] This diversified their content offering, attracting a new audience and creating additional revenue streams through podcast advertising.

---

[15] Ek, Daniel. "Audio-First — Spotify." February 6, 2019. Accessed June 21, 2025. https://newsroom.spotify.com/2019-02-06/audio-first/

desirability
(people)

viability
(business)

feasibility
(technology)

Innovation sweet spot

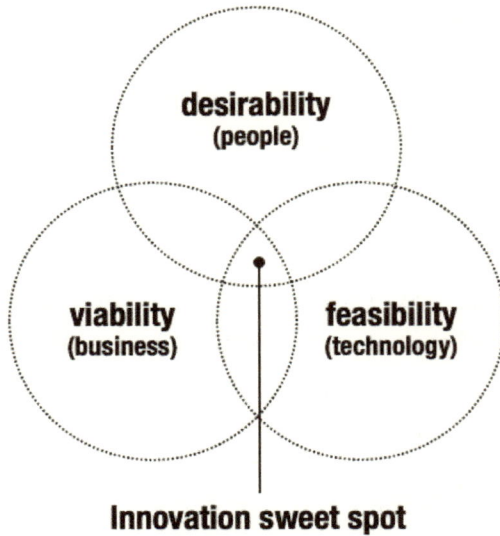

The art and science of innovation is an iterative problem-solving process that integrates what IDEO famously calls the three lenses of design thinking: people, technology, and business.[16] To truly innovate, you must combine these elements, resulting in a product or service that hits the sweet spot of viability (generating profit), desirability (meeting user needs and wants), and feasibility (being technically achievable). As a design leader, collaborating closely with your business and technology partners is absolutely essential to making this a reality and ensuring you effectively champion your unique piece of the innovation pie: the voice of the customer.

---

[16] "What is Design Thinking? — updated 2024." *IxDF*. May 25, 2016. Accessed June 21, 2025. https://www.interaction-design.org/literature/topics/design-thinking

Customer Centricity

As the customer advocate and user champion, you have a unique opportunity to embed customer obsession into the very DNA of your company. By embracing User-Centered Design (UCD), and with the necessary time and support, each step outlined below will empower you to influence decision-making and elevate collaboration by actively involving users throughout the design process.

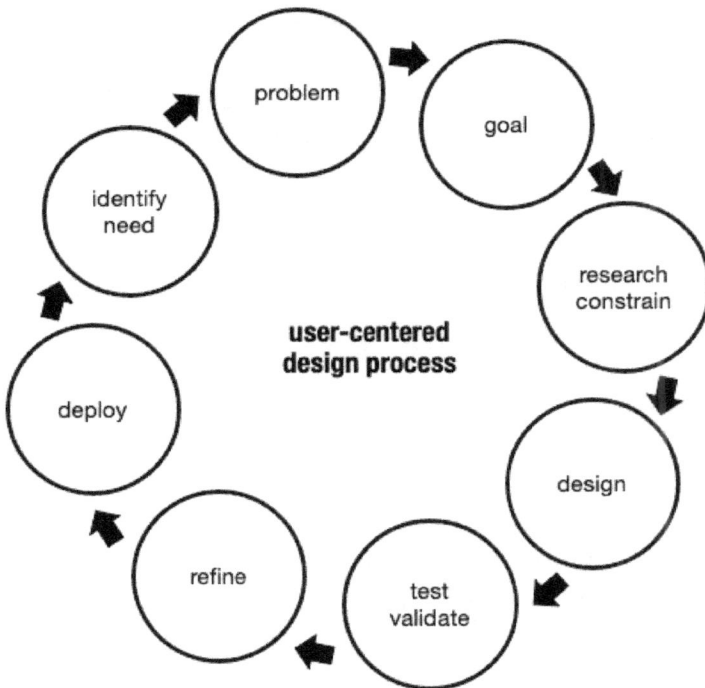

- **Goal**: Define the overarching objective or desired outcome that the product aims to achieve for the user and the business.

- **Research/Constrain:** Gather information about users, their context, and existing solutions, while also understanding any technical, business, or resource limitations.

- **Design:** Create concepts, wireframes, prototypes, and visual interfaces based on insights from research and defined goals.

- **Test/Validate:** Put prototypes or early versions of the product design in front of actual users to observe their interactions and gather feedback.

- **Refine:** Iterate on the product design based on feedback from testing and validation, making improvements to enhance usability and effectiveness.

- **Deploy:** Launch or implement the finalized product design for users to interact with in a real-world environment.

- **Identify Need:** Discover and clearly articulate the fundamental problems, desires, or unfulfilled requirements of the target users.

- **Problem**: Clearly define the specific challenge or pain point that the product design solution aims to address for the target audience.

UCD Case Study: Online News Site Redesign

In 2003, I led the redesign of Yahoo News. The News team's goals included identifying which readers were engaging most and for what reasons. By understanding who our target audience was, we could create a personalized experience, which would encourage more readers and more time spent on the news site. With increased reader growth, we could attract better, more targeted advertisers and increase ad revenue.

To understand our target customers, we collaborated with the market research team and conducted focus groups and user surveys to gauge existing readers' sentiments about the website. We saw that several segments of readers shared similar sentiments. For example, one group preferred their news to be well-organized, quick to navigate, and characterized by unbiased storytelling.

Next, we took samples from each segment. We combined the focus group results with quantitative research conducted by a third-party research company to identify the level of engagement each segment exhibited in reading news online. Each segment was linked to business metrics, such as the most active news readers, the time they spent reading news, how frequently they visit, and where else they might seek news sources.

One target customer segment we named the 'informed citizen' who strives to stay informed about current events, values diverse perspectives, and forms well-informed opinions to share with others. We investigated each segment employing ethnographic research to uncover hidden needs and behaviors within each segment. Our research methods included user journey mapping to visualize the customer experience of our own news app and those of our competitors, to discover any pain points.

We used personas (archetypal user representations) to inform our design thinking, validate our assumptions and gather feedback on the new site prototypes we were developing. Our marketing team provided data analytics for each segment, giving us a holistic view of the various target customer segments and identifying those whose needs, if met, could yield the most rewards.

Our 'informed citizen' was emerging as a strong candidate– busy professionals who valued efficiency in their news consumption, utilizing multiple online sources to gather information quickly. They seek a human element in news, looking for emotional stories that resonate with them. They are skeptical of any single news source and believe in the importance of cross-referencing information.

We brainstormed ideas, creating storyboards that took the persona and data into concepts that illustrated what providing related stories or emotional stories might be like. We also planned to make it easy for them to join an online community of news readers, allowing them to stay connected with others.

As the ideal target customer emerged from our combined qualitative and quantitative research and guided the development of personalized product features and findings, it was a unifying and exciting experience for the entire News team. Within a year of its launch, our redesign became the most visited U.S. news website, attracting five times more customers or 'traffic' than before.

Execution

The most brilliant design ideas are worthless if they cannot be built. The ability to lead your team through the entire design and development process to execution is vital. When you consistently deliver high-quality, executable designs, you build credibility and trust across engineering, product, and business teams, enabling you to influence strategic decisions more effectively. You likely know all this already, but here are four actions you can take to help your teams become more proficient at execution.[17]

Create and Share Unified Design Systems: Establish a centralized platform to house and manage all design strategies, user research insights, and project initiatives. This ensures a unified design vision across product teams, fostering consistency and eliminating design silos. This information would be linked and accessible through a company intranet or a dedicated design team webpage, ensuring your cross-functional partners stay aligned with you!

Track User Interaction Data: You can gather feedback by leveraging dashboards such as Google Analytics or Adobe Analytics for web analytics or InVision Analytics to monitor user interaction with prototypes. If you don't have dedicated user researchers, there are plenty of apps to help you record, review, and analyze user testing feedback or track user behavior on mobile apps.

Enhance XFN Collaboration: Use collaborative design tools and communication platforms to enhance teamwork across design, product, and engineering teams. This way, you can facilitate design critiques, share user research findings, and track design progress within a shared workspace between design, development, and product management. Two well-known collaboration applications are Figma and Miro, an online whiteboard and collaboration platform.

---

[17] O, "Scott. "Step-by-Step Strategic Execution Guide." August 20, 2024. Accessed May 5, 2025. https://www.spiderstrategies.com/blog/strategic-execution/

Consistent Automated Reporting: Provides a real-time pulse on the user experience. The benefit of doing this is that it frees your teams to concentrate on creative problem-solving while ensuring consistent reporting on design progress. Depending on what you need to report on, there are tools that are integrated directly into your website or app. that automatically collect quantitative UX data without manual intervention. Additionally, there are specialized data visualization tools (like Looker Studio, Power BI, and Tableau) that can be configured to send automated alerts when key UX performance indicators deviate from expected thresholds, enabling proactive problem identification and faster responses.

Your Impact Across the Tech Landscape

Whether you're navigating the whirlwind of a nascent startup, where every design decision feels monumental, or contributing within the established structures of a mature organization, each tech company growth stage presents distinct opportunities and challenges for your leadership, directly shaped by how design is integrated and leveraged for the customer.

Perhaps you thrive in the fast-paced, high-stakes environment of a scrappy startup, where you can directly shape the foundational user experience, or maybe you're drawn to the resources and expansive scale of a growth-stage company, where you can influence product strategy across a broad user base. You might even find yourself fortunate enough to ride the exhilarating waves of both within the same organization. Over time, you'll know where your skills and passions best align.

To help you discover your ideal work environment, we're going to break down the lifecycle of a tech startup and focus specifically on the role of design in each stage.

> *"Someone's sitting in the shade today because someone planted a tree a long time ago."*
> *Warren Buffett*

To Begin: Pre-Seed Stage

This is the beginning where the business ideas are just taking shape, and no significant revenue has been generated. There may be a minimal or non-existent user base or market traction.[18] The people working there are usually a team of founders looking for initial funding to validate their idea, build a prototype, and conduct market research. Unless one of the founders has some design skills and experience bootstrapping design, hiring a full-time designer or researcher is unlikely. Contract help is more likely to be brought in to translate business concepts into prototypes, gather user feedback, build a small user base, and help the founders acquire seed funding for further development. If working at a pre-seed startup is of interest to you,

Ask Yourself

- What is your philosophy on the role of design at this early stage, and how do you envision design influencing key strategic decisions beyond just the user interface?

---

[18] Sullivan, Kaylin. "Pre-seed funding: What it is and how to get it." *SeedLegals.* September 28, 2022. Accessed May 5, 2025. https://seedlegals.com/resources/pre-seed-funding/

- How do you plan to validate your core assumptions about the problem, the solution, and the target users? What role will design play in leading or facilitating this validation process?

- What is your operational rhythm and decision-making process, especially when faced with uncertainty or conflicting opinions? How will design be integrated into your day-to-day workflow and communication?

Attracting Funding: Seed Stage

Seed-stage startups are in the nascent development phase, where executives the focus is on establishing a business strategy to achieve product-market fit.[19] The goal is to prove to investors that there is market demand for their products. The founders and a few key employees will build a minimum viable product (MVP) to attract funding from angel investors, venture capitalists, or crowdfunding platforms. Adding a full-time user experience designer to encompass all aspects of the end-user interaction and prototyping would be an ideal hire at this stage.

Ask Yourself

- What does the MVP truly entail, and how will design define its core user experience to demonstrate value? (Are we building just enough to learn, or too much too soon?)

---

[19] "Stages of startups: YC Startup Job Guide." *Y Combinator*. Accessed May 5, 2025. https://www.ycombinator.com/library/Ek-stages-of-startups

- How will design contribute directly to the fundraising narrative and pitch deck? (Am I expected to create content to tell the product story to investors?)

- What autonomy will I have to conduct user research, define user flows, and prototype solutions? (Will I be empowered to truly lead design decisions?)

- What is the runway, and how will the initial funding be used? (Will there be enough resources to conduct meaningful design work and user validation?)

Validating Tech: Growth Stage (Series A)

At this stage, the startup has moved to a growth stage, and the financial backing to pursue its goals. Series A funding, typically more than $10 million validates the company's potential. It attracts further attention from investors and the broader market.[20] The capital infusion enables the startup to expand its team, scale operations, and invest in marketing and sales efforts. Including a Head of Design who can hire contract or full-time individuals to research, design, test, prototype, and build a brand would help it achieve its goals. You will wear many hats in this role, both hands-on and strategic.

---

[20] "How to Crush Your Series A Funding Goals." *Verified Metrics*. Accessed May 5, 2025. https://www.verifiedmetrics.com/blog/how-to-crush-your-series-a-funding-goals

Ask Yourself

- What are the top 3-5 product priorities for the next 6-12 months, and how does design fit into achieving them? (Understand the strategic roadmap and your alignment).

- What are the key business metrics and how do they relate to product usage? (Shows their business acumen and how design can directly impact revenue).

- Who are the main competitors, and what is our unique differentiator from a user experience perspective? (Helps you position the product and your design strategy).

- How do product, engineering, and design collaborate on a day-to-day basis? (Reveals the collaboration maturity and potential friction points).

Scaling Up: Growth Stage (Series B)

Companies that attain Series B funding focus on scaling existing operations, expanding market share, and building a strong foundation for future growth. Key objectives include further solidifying product-market fit through aggressive customer acquisition and retention strategies.[21] Scaling operations while maintaining profitability and controlling costs achieves operational efficiency. Attracting and retaining top talent across all departments helps expand into new markets, and investing in product development drives continued growth.

---

[21] "What Is Series B Funding: Steps for Expanding the Business." *Cloudvisor*. October 26, 2024. Accessed May 5, 2025. https://cloudvisor.co/blog/what-is-series-b-funding/

As a design leader, you can build and expand a core team of creative individuals who will drive the company's success. While funding may be available, securing headcount can be challenging, especially when competing with revenue-generating departments like sales and marketing. To effectively advocate for your team's growth, it's essential to deeply understand the organization's business goals and how they are measured and to demonstrate how your design outcomes directly contribute to achieving these objectives. This is where a strong understanding of the business strategy is paramount.

Ask Yourself

- What is the current design maturity of the company? (e.g., Is design primarily seen as UI/UX, or is it integrated into product strategy? Are there existing design systems, research practices, etc.?)

- What are the immediate and long-term product roadmap goals? How will design contribute to achieving these?

- What is the relationship between design, product, and engineering? Is it harmonious or siloed? How will you foster strong cross-functional collaboration?

- What is the budget allocation for design (tooling, research, hiring, professional development)? Is it sufficient for the ambitious growth plans?

- What is my leadership philosophy, and how does it align with the company's values?

Maturing the Company: The Growth Stage (Series C)

As a company reaches its Series C funding round, the focus shifts dramatically towards maximizing market dominance, achieving sustainable profitability, and meticulously preparing for a successful exit, whether through an Initial Public Offering (IPO) or an acquisition. Key business objectives at this stage include aggressive market expansion, like entering new territories, strategically acquiring competitors, and making substantial investments in research and development to solidify a competitive edge. Concurrently, the emphasis is on scaling operations to meet increased demand and optimizing efficiency across the board. Growth-stage tech companies are also actively strengthening their financial position to attract potential buyers or present an attractive profile for an IPO.

Your role in preparing for the future is to scale how you work and what you deliver, ensuring consistency and predictability in direct alignment with the company's business objectives. This means proactively optimizing and streamlining essential processes like hiring and talent retention within your teams. You'll be instrumental in codifying design processes, refining design reviews, and perfecting user testing and feedback cycles to ensure a smooth, high-quality output. Staying ahead of emerging technology and design trends, ensuring that your company's design language and brand identity remain adaptable and future-proof. By focusing on these areas, you're actively preparing your teams—and the entire company—for the demands of an even larger scale and a successful future.

Ask Yourself

- What design systems, processes, and tools are currently in place? (Is there a shared component library? What's the typical design-to-development handoff process? What tools are used for collaboration?)

- What new markets, user segments, or product lines are being considered, and how will design inform these expansions?

- How does the design team currently collaborate with product management and engineering? (Are workflows smooth? Are there common points of friction? How are disagreements resolved?)

- What opportunities are there for me to influence the broader company culture and operations beyond the design function?

"After going public, the focus shifted dramatically."
Phil Clevenger

Transforming the Company: Exit Stage

This is the final stage, and the focus shifts from hyper-growth to ensuring a smooth transition. How the company exits will depend on the founder's goals, but there are three main ways to exit: selling the founder's shares to another company, acquiring another company, or holding an Initial Public Offering (IPO). As a design leader, you can take steps to prepare the company for an exit by ensuring that its design systems, processes, and documentation are well-organized and easily accessible for due diligence. Taking the initiative to communicate customer-informed, data-driven case studies will strengthen your argument for maintaining your teams and preventing layoffs during the typical cost-reduction phase that companies often undertake to enhance their attractiveness to buyers and shareholders.

Ask Yourself

- How will the exit impact the existing product roadmap and the priorities for design moving forward? Will there be significant shifts or a continuation of current plans?

- What is the current structure and size of the design team, and what are the plans for its growth or restructuring post-exit?

- How will design leadership contribute to executive-level strategic decisions? Will there be a seat at the table for design at the highest levels?

- What is the culture of the acquiring company (if applicable), and how does it align with the existing design culture? Are there significant differences that might impact the team?

The DNA of a tech company is profoundly influenced by design leaders who champion a user-centered and agile approach to development, fostering innovation, collaboration, customer centricity, and efficient execution. To bring these principles to life and demonstrate how a design leader can navigate and thrive within such an environment, we turn to the invaluable insights of Rob Girling. As a seasoned design professional who has not only built his own successful company, Artefact, but also held significant product design leadership roles at major tech giants.

EXECUTIVE INSIGHT WITH ROB GIRLING

Robert Girling is a design leader with a distinguished background. A Fellow of the Royal Society of Arts (FRSA) and graduate of the prestigious Royal College of Art (RCA), Rob's career has spanned design giants such as IDEO, Sony Entertainment, Microsoft, and Apple. Leveraging his expertise in user experience design, Rob co-founded Artefact, a Seattle-based consultancy focused on purpose-driven strategy and design. Here, Rob's vision for better managing project resources materialized.

The Birth of 10,000ft: A Solution Bred From Need

In 2011, Rob co-founded 10,000ft, a resource management application initially developed within Artefact to streamline its internal operations. This innovative tool aimed to provide a clear "big-picture" view (hence the name referencing the high altitude) for managing teams, projects, and client work.

10,000ft's intuitive design and functionality resonated beyond Artefact. The software's success led to its acquisition by Smartsheet in 2017. Fast forward to 2024, and 10,000ft became part of an $8.4 billion acquisition of Smartsheet by Blackstone and Vista Equity Partners.

The Author's Connection with 10,000ft

The story of 10,000ft holds particular significance for me because I used it when I was Chief Design Officer to coordinate the work of three design teams in India, the Philippines, and the USA. Beyond its beautiful interface, the software offered exceptional transparency into our project workflows, fostering collaboration across borders. It felt custom-designed for us, which, as it turns out, wasn't far from the truth! Here is the inspiring origin story of 10,000ft from my interview with Rob Girling.

10,000ft Origin Story

Myself, Gavin Kelly, Artefact's co-founder, and Martijn van Tilburg had all met and spent around 10 years at Microsoft, where we climbed the ranks to mid-level management, soaking up the Microsoft DNA. Having experienced that firsthand, we felt pretty confident in our ability to build and launch products.

In 2006, the tech world was still riding a wave of excitement, especially in the design community. We were all optimistic and excited about the potential for design to shape the future of technology. It felt like design was riding a wave, building on the legacy of IDEO and other pioneers in the field, and so we began Artefact, a product design consultancy.

At the time, there was a real sense that working in product innovation was magic. We could brainstorm, conceive, 3D print, hack some sensors, and, with some cleverness, produce a snazzy working prototype in an incredibly short space of time. It felt real, tangible, and incredibly exciting. We were all caught up in this wave of optimism, thinking, "If we can build these cool prototypes, surely shipping a product can't be that hard." Of course, as the story unfolds, we soon realize just how wrong we were.

Learning From Failure

Between 2006 and 2011, we experimented with various product concepts, working with industrial designers and skilled engineers to create impressive prototypes. It was easy to get caught up in the excitement, imagining these prototypes as future realities. We even launched a few Kickstarter campaigns, but unfortunately, we didn't get enough traction.

Each failed attempt was a valuable lesson. We learned from our mistakes and pushed the boundaries of what was possible. The spark for 10,000ft ignited when Martin, the future CEO, grew weary of consulting. He proposed building some kind of SaaS business software and productivity tool, but web-based and modern.

We had, by that time, already learned a valuable lesson: Do what you know. It's like the writing adage, 'Write what you know,' but applied to design. Design something you deeply understand. At Artefact Consulting, with around 30 people, we faced a common challenge: tracking projects, budgets, and team allocations. It was a problem we knew intimately. It worked in a spreadsheet up to about 20 people, but then it started getting really clunky. So, in January 2012, several of us sat down and decided to build a resource management tool for designers. We didn't have a grand vision at the start, but shortly into the project, it became clear that supporting creative teams had something potentially valuable to offer other organizations.

Building an Audience

Initially, we thought our target audience would be similar design companies. But soon, a bigger idea emerged: the world was shifting toward teams and distributed organizations facing the challenge of an increasingly creative workforce who craved more autonomy and creativity. Rather than a tool that would just help them track routine tasks, we prioritized this outcome: "Let's allocate the right talented resources, figure out a budget, and trust the team to figure out the details." Our hope was that users wanted tools that unlocked their creative energy and not ones that micromanaged their time and task load to the nth degree. It was unclear to us if 'customers' would pay for that, but we knew that, as users ourselves, we wanted it.

Within six months, around June of 2012, we had a functional prototype—a bit of a hack, to be honest. Our amazing engineering team quickly compiled a web UI, timeline view, and basic management features. And we were using it at Artefact within six months of that first sitting-down meeting. It felt pretty good. All that was left was that small task of announcing ourselves to the world, selling it, and supporting it. (Hah!)

Meeting with the Press

At that point, we had just hired a marketing manager, Adriana Gil Miner, a new talent at Artefact. We'd never had anyone in marketing before, but we had a very capable someone now. She helped us craft a message about what we were doing and figure out how to get the word out through PR, reaching out to various media figures, including Mark Wilson, head of global design innovation at Fast Company at the time.[22] He wrote about 10,000ft and was incredibly enthusiastic. Liz Stinson at Wired wrote, "We've heard a lot about the importance of design in business, and tools like 10,000ft are manifestations of that new focus."[23]

After succeeding in getting the word out to some degree, within a month or two of launching our beta, we had twenty design agencies and companies using trial versions worldwide. We hadn't even set up payment and accounts infrastructure or hired a support team. It was chaotic, but we really believed in the reality of a testing market fit before fully polishing the offering. Fortunately, we had plenty of designers and developers at Artefact to lend a hand. But we were seriously lacking in other areas.

It was a pretty chaotic situation. The 10,000ft team moved into demo sell mode, constantly pitching the

---

[22] "Fastcompany.com." Accessed May 5, 2025. https://www.fastcompany.com/1670069/a-project-management-tool-built-for-some-of-the-countrys-best-design-firms

[23] Stinson, Liz. "This New Tool Helps Designers Find Better Insights." *WIRED.* September 24, 2015. Accessed May 5, 2025. https://www.wired.com/2015/09/new-tool-helps-designers-find-better-insights/

product to potential customers and hearing their feedback whilst constantly getting feedback from actual trial users.

We were pushing this product without fully understanding the complexities of launching, but with a certain degree of confidence that we could figure it out. Slowly, it began to dawn on us that while we had extensive experience at the front end of the product conception and development process, we had collectively very little experience with the intricate complexities of the marketing, selling, and support side of the product development process. Even pricing strategy, a key element, was something we'd really neglected to consider in any detail.

We realized that many design companies aspire to build products, but few had actually succeeded at that time. It's a tough challenge, especially for service-based organizations that rely on hourly rates. One major hurdle is the significant revenue difference between selling time and selling a product. The short-term revenue opportunity is always going to distract resources away from the potential of more long-term product revenue.

Paying Its Own Way

We separated 10,000ft and Artefact into two organizations prior to launch so that employees were dedicated to 10,000ft and were working from a budget we'd allocated to the project. Artefact could also offer consulting team members to the project at a 'cost rate,' which helped in those first few months/years enormously. That limited runway basically forced 10000ft to become financially viable really quickly, needing to earn enough money to cover most or all of its own expenses. We all believed that bootstrapping was better than scaling or seeking outsider investor money. Bootstrapping basically means that every time we signed on a new customer, it gave us X amount of booked revenue for the future, which allowed us to grow. Within a few months, customers committed to early product pricing contracts, and the whole thing started to scale up.

By early 2013, we hit a key transition point, where incoming revenue covered all ongoing expenses. Some employees of the new organization took some equity to reduce expenses, but the business was on the long, slow scaling process that many SaaS startups face.

What's in a Name?

The name 10,000ft came from a brainstorm where everybody was involved. I don't remember who came up with the specific suggestion. Martijn, I think, designed the logo. His idea for a hot air balloon and logotype using numbers was a genius move. With the number 1 in the title, the product's name was guaranteed to appear at the very top of any listing of companies.

It's hard to pinpoint exactly who deserves credit for the user interface and experience design. It is safest to say it was a group effort, but Martijn was in charge of all the executive design and experience decisions. There was no shortage of contributing voices and feedback and endless iteration. We had only three or so software engineers at the start, who were also incredible at quickly turning designs into reality. Two of the founding contributors, the head of engineering and one of the UX designers, ended up staying with the product and are still working on it today.

Organizational Design

Unlike many other companies, Artefact took an unconventional approach to hiring and management. We hired people who we believed to be highly capable, and those who couldn't quickly adapt to our fast-paced environment didn't last long. We inherited a bit of Microsoft's 'sync or swim' mentality, where everyone was expected to be in sync and highly responsive.

Our philosophy was to empower individuals and eliminate traditional hierarchies. One novel idea at the time was that we believed nobody wanted managers; they wanted feedback. So early at Artefact, people were assigned coaches. Unlike managers, who are typically around to task you and give you performance feedback and ratings, our coaches' goal was to support you with whatever task you were doing, give you feedback, and be a sounding board for ideas. We set clear objectives and outcomes, but there was no micromanagement. Instead, coaches offered guidance and support without formal performance reviews. This approach fostered a culture of autonomy and innovation.

Artefact became a very flat organization, and it worked pretty well. Unsurprisingly, that cultural DNA (flat management and total transparency) found its way into the initial design of 10000 ft.

Meeting Customer Needs

A year or two in, we began to attract larger, non-design-related clients. The timeline view resonated with our marketing and product demos. It's clear, easy to understand, and visually appealing. Plus, the idea of easily making changes and adjustments was attractive. Originally built for our own needs, it naturally integrated design principles, and the allure of a more open and employee-empowering approach was strong.

Everyone aspires to be a company with high trust, employee empowerment, and autonomy. Even though they might not fully grasp the challenges of implementing such a culture, the idea is appealing. Our product seemed to fit that idea, but still, there would come a moment inevitably in the demos or trials of 10000ft when we noticed a sense of customer apprehension about the product's articulation of workplace transparency.

Larger organizations typically hesitated to share details about vacation schedules, resource allocation, and projects running 'hot.' Potential buyers in larger companies wanted tight controls over who had the power to set up, change, and manage projects, all a bit counter to our initial ideas. For example, determining who has the authority to modify a plan is a critical decision. Our initial egalitarian approach, while transparent, presented challenges, especially in scenarios where changes were made without proper oversight. It became clear that wasn't going to fly in some larger organizations. We needed strict permissions regarding who could change what, who was in charge of what, and how many changes could be made before someone was notified.

Time tracking was seen in some organizations as a kind of organizational surveillance mechanism over the employee. Employees would feel pressure to enter data that reflected what they thought management expected, rather than risk being exposed for spending too long on something or being cast as inefficient. Managers saw time tracking as the only way to tell if things were on budget and on time. Instead of focusing on specific numbers and rigid time tracking, we adopted a more flexible and trust-based approach. We recognized that micromanagement was counterproductive and that a certain level of autonomy was essential for productivity.

Needless to say, as the product matured, it grew to accommodate many different work-culture practices and organizational preferences, but we managed to hold onto something of that original empowering concept with the choice of default preferences.

It took a couple of years to win the bigger customers. There were a couple of reasons for that. The biggest initial challenge was that the original super prototype we built wasn't at all performant for larger teams. Early on, we'd sacrificed scalability and flexibility for getting to market as quickly as possible, and in doing so, incurred a large engineering debt. A large amount of time was spent post-launch rebuilding the entire product whilst it was already, in many cases, deployed to paying customers.

Larger customers also had sophisticated Six Sigma reliability expectations, a need to support hundreds of team members, and a need for round-the-clock support. They also demanded sophisticated administrative controls and interoperability with existing systems.

These practical considerations, such as maintenance, administrative panels, security, and customized permissions for each organization, were crucial for real-world implementation. All the kinds of stuff that we honestly had no interest in, but were essential to support larger companies.

Growing the Team

We launched in 2012, and by 2016, 10,000ft had grown to a team of around 35 full-time folks. We had spent years building up a small support, marketing, and sales team. Maintaining growing sales became an ongoing challenge after the first couple of years.

Reaching and winning mid-size or large organizations is a long, drawn-out sales process that requires huge time investments. Compared to smaller clients, the cost of acquiring each new client becomes larger and larger. The team would have to constantly juggle decisions: How much should we spend on marketing, sales, and development? Should we prioritize a complete product or continuous innovation? Should we take outside money to massively grow our sales game? Many SaaS companies face this balancing act.

Month after month, we monitored trends, and everything was moving up and to the right, as they say. But inevitably, there were those lulls, those periods of relative quiet when new deals seemed elusive. It was a constant worry: Had we reached our peak? Had some competitor offering a new feature trumped our momentum? It's the standard anxiety that comes with managing a product, let alone the difficulties of keeping team morale up and everyone focused.

Our Exit Strategy

At a key offsite in 2011, we asked ourselves two crucial questions: "Why do this?" and "If we build a product, what's the exit plan?"

Looking back at when we embarked on this journey, we remembered how we were driven by the belief that we could create something truly innovative and special and that we'd prove something to ourselves, learn how to be a fully rounded product thinker, and have a lot of fun along the way.

As to what the exit plan was, two key ideas emerged.

The first potential exit was a steady stream of revenue. A long-term product deal would provide a consistent income stream, unlike the unpredictable nature of consulting projects. This stability would allow us (Artefact) to balance the peaks and troughs inherent in consultancy, creating a more sustainable business model and allowing us to invest in real thought leadership and potentially other product opportunities.

A second, a potential exit could be building the product, scaling it, and eventually selling it for a significant return. This was a more ambitious but potentially lucrative path. While I was initially drawn to the first vision—a sustainable, product-focused company—the reality of building and scaling a product is far more complex. It requires significant investment, a dedicated team, and a clear market opportunity.

The first model was an unrealistic yet idealistic vision, mostly confounded by the desire to keep the resources, product efforts, budgets, and legal agreements separate. So the question became, when is 'big enough,' big enough to go to market?

By 2017, the product was already generating significant profits, all of which were being funneled back into the company as continued growth capital. SaaS companies like ours started to be interesting acquisition targets to buyers at a certain revenue size, and our internal conversation became fairly focused on how, when we hit that number, we would see if anyone was interested in purchasing us.

When we finally did hit that revenue number, we had a full marketing plan ready to go, including a list of potential buyers, but just as we were about to go to market (I think the day before), we were approached by SmartSheet. We asked ourselves if we were happy with their offer, and after a bit of negotiation, we voted unanimously to accept.

Everyone, except for Martijn, the CEO, went to work for Smartsheet. This wasn't unusual and not a reflection on him in any way. Smartsheet explained that they didn't see the acquisition as a bolt-on organization; they wanted to integrate it fully into their existing organization, offerings, and strategies. Thus, the need for the visionary founder was no longer key.[24]

Overall, we had a very pleasant experience with the CEO, CFO, and other executives at Smartsheet. It wasn't the cutthroat deal-making we'd been led to believe was typical of acquisitions. They were a very decent bunch, very reasonable, and it seemed like a great fit. The sale went very smoothly.[25]

Interestingly, and a nice little anecdote is that SmartSheet continued to employ many of the original 10,000ft employees, a testament to being a great employer in its own right. Recently, they sold the company for $8.4 billion. Many of our former colleagues who joined them received equity, so I'm sure they got a nice bonus.

There were times over those six or seven years when the three of us on the board would argue about whether to take outside investment or continue the bootstrapping strategy. Endless stories of Silicon Valley unicorns, massive

---

[24] "Artefact spinoff launches first product: 10,000ft helps manage projects, people" *GeekWire.* Accessed May 5, 2025. https://www.geekwire.com/2012/artefact-spinoff-launches-first-product-10000ft-software-for-managing-projects-people/

[25] "10,000Ft." *Industrial Designers Society of America.* Accessed May 5, 2025. https://www.idsa.org/awards-recognition/idea/idea-gallery/10000ft/

investments, and huge sales teams served as constant distractions, making our efforts and rather conservative growth strategy seem a bit quaint. Having the patience to not flood the company with outsider cash and lose control to people who only cared about the bottom line took a great deal of restraint and commitment to the idea that we were in it for more than just the money.

We cared about the team, were passionate about the product (perhaps in a way that you don't see outside of design circles much anymore), and were interested in our own personal growth as much as anything. So, looking back, I'm proud of our patience and that we didn't fall out as friends. I think this owes a lot to Martijn's personality and his vision as a CEO. It's gratifying that our people-centered design vision was a successful strategy. I'm truly proud of that. Perhaps the biggest growth we experienced was despite knowing how to create a great product; we knew very little about the complexities of sales and other aspects of product development. A few years into the project, 10,000ft had shaped our attitudes at Artefact.[26] We now understand the challenges of building firsthand and have developed more empathy for our customers. We weren't those arrogant designers anymore, showing off potential concepts with no sense of how hard they would be to forge into businesses.

---

[26] Wilson, Mark. "10,000ft | Planning and collaboration for creative teams." *Artefact*. Accessed May 5, 2025. https://www.artefactgroup.com/case-studies/10000ft-10000ft-insights/

Having 10,000ft on Artefact's case studies deck has earned us legitimacy because we have built, sold, and seen the success of our own product.

CHAPTER 4

Your Role in Corporate Strategy

DECODING CORPORATE STRATEGY FOR DESIGN LEADERS

For a design leader, understanding corporate strategy is the key to elevating design's influence within the tech landscape. This chapter demystifies the 'big picture' planning that shapes a company's long-term trajectory, revealing how C-suite executives craft strategic visions and allocate resources. We'll explore how you can forge strong alignment with this decision-making level, grasping the metrics and priorities that drive their actions. We'll also examine essential corporate strategies relevant to design in tech, offering actionable insights into aligning your team's efforts with overarching business goals. To solidify these concepts with a tangible example, the concluding section of this chapter features insights from Julie Baher, VP at Myriad Genetics. She offers a real-world perspective on how corporate strategy directly shapes the responsibilities and impact of design leadership within this genetic testing and precision medicine company.

WHAT IS CORPORATE STRATEGY?

Corporate strategy is a high-level plan that outlines a company's long-term goals, objectives, and the competitive advantages it aims to achieve.[27] It serves as the company's blueprint or 'big picture' and addresses questions such as:

- What businesses should we pursue?

- How should we allocate resources among these businesses?

- How do we create value across the entire corporation?

For example, Netflix's corporate strategy is to "entertain the world," and their vision is to be the world's leading internet entertainment service. To achieve this, Netflix focuses on a vast content library, seamless integration across all devices, and personalized user experiences, all for a subscription price. They invest heavily in making their shows and have added ads and games. This 'big picture' corporate strategy guides every major decision Netflix makes, from content to ads, and how they allocate their resources, setting the stage for how their design teams build their products.

---

[27] Lastiri, Lorea. "9 Reasons Why Corporate Strategy Matters (w/Practical Tips)." *Kippy*. June 11, 2023. Accessed April 29, 2025. https://www.kippy.cloud/post/reasons-why-corporate-strategy-matters

WHO CREATES CORPORATE STRATEGY?

Key players in shaping corporate strategy include the founders, executive leaders, and investors, such as private equity firms, angel investors, family investors, and venture capitalists. The executive team, typically led by the CEO, serves as the primary driver of the organization. This section outlines the roles and responsibilities of key C-suite members and offers suggestions for understanding, aligning with, and collaborating with keepers of corporate strategy.

Chief Executive Officer (CEO)

A CEO's role is to guide the company's growth and establish it as a leader within its industry. The responsibilities are numerous, diverse, and often unpredictable. They may include overseeing expansion plans and operations, coordinating teams, building a strong executive group, nurturing relationships with the board and investors, allocating resources, mitigating risks, and inspiring employees to achieve the company's objectives.

As a design executive, your interactions with the CEO may depend on the company's size. Your connection with the CEO may be significant at a startup. However, at a mature tech company your exposure to the CEO might be indirect, through attending all-hands meetings, company events, or presentations you receive or deliver. I never spoke directly to Terry Semel, Yahoo's CEO from 2001 to 2007, but I remember him interviewing Tom Cruise and Katie Holmes at our campus headquarters in Sunnyvale, CA. Terry's and Tom's families vacationed together regularly and shared anecdotes from their holidays spent swimming off Terry's yacht at his vacation home in Miami. Tom and Terry had an excellent rapport, starkly contrasting with the tech duo of Jerry Yang and David Filo, the company's founders. They transformed a web directory into a global internet powerhouse. David's background in electrical engineering infused a 'do-it-yourself' entrepreneurial spirit and a focus on user experience and innovation. By contrast, Jerry brought a pragmatic, business-oriented approach to tech. He was open and available for meetings, and when he told me that the company's corporate strategy was to aggregate content. When I heard this, I felt I had been given a key to the palace and a map to the top of the mountain. This clarity helped me have the confidence to question anything that did not align with it. To help you feel confident in your dealings with the C-team, who can, let's face it, seem like scary dudes, here are tailored questions you can ask so you can show your stuff, build rapport, and like Jerry did for me, give you the keys to understanding corporate strategy.

Questions for Your CEO

- "How do we currently measure the success of our product and user experience, and what data, both quantitative and qualitative, is most valuable to you in understanding our customers?"

This question directly addresses how design impact is viewed and measured within the company. It reveals the CEO's existing understanding of customer needs and the data points they prioritize. It also hints at the availability and maturity of user research and analytics within the organization.

- "What is the single biggest unmet need or pain point our customers experience with our current offerings, and how do you envision design specifically addressing that in the next 12-18 months?"

This forces the CEO to articulate a specific, high-impact problem. It helps you understand the CEO's strategic priorities for product evolution and where they believe design can make the most significant difference. It also sets an early expectation for how design will contribute to solving key business challenges.

- "How would you describe our company's core values and unique differentiation in the market, and how do you believe our product experience currently embodies (or fails to embody) those attributes?"

This question delves into the company's DNA and brand identity. Understanding the core values helps ensure your design decisions reinforce the brand. Asking how the product experience reflects these values (or not) can reveal disconnects that design can help bridge, and also indicates the CEO's level of self-awareness about their product's current standing.

- "What are the biggest internal challenges or roadblocks you foresee that might hinder our ability to innovate and deliver exceptional user experiences, and how can design leadership help overcome them?"

This proactively uncovers potential organizational friction points (e.g., Silos, resource constraints, technological debt, cultural issues) that could impact your effectiveness. It also positions you as a strategic partner, looking to contribute beyond design and help improve operational efficiency and collaboration.

Chief Technical Officer (CTO)

The CTO outlines the 'how' of technology, while you, as the design leader for the company, focus on the 'why' of user experience design (UXD).[28] The CTO's role in corporate strategy involves developing a technology roadmap that includes a long-term vision, architecture, and standards. They manage the IT infrastructure, lead technology teams, ensure the security and privacy of the company's systems and data, explore emerging technologies to drive business growth and innovation, and oversee the development and launch of new products and services.

According to Ajay Thakur, head of cognitive computing at Uber, "A good designer knows what is feasible within our engineering limitations and can provide constructive pushback to ensure we strive for maximum utility in our products."

To move toward working effectively with your CTO, you could start by asking them these questions.

Questions for your CTO

- "How does our current tech stack support our long-term product vision, and what are the most significant technical debt areas we need to address to get there?"

---

[28] Woollacott, Emma. "What Is A Chief Technology Officer? CTO Role Explained." Accessed April 29, 2025. https://www.forbes.com/sites/emmawoollacott/article/chief-technology-officer-cto/

This question immediately connects your strategic goals with engineering's realities. It probes for the "how" of alignment and surfaces potential roadblocks (technical debt) that will impact your design team's ability to innovate and deliver on future experiences. It's crucial for understanding the current capabilities and limitations.

- "What are the key architectural principles and design patterns that underpin our core platforms, and how do they impact our ability to iterate quickly and build scalable, resilient user experiences?"

This delves into the 'what' of the fundamental structure. Understanding architecture helps you grasp the underlying logic, flexibility, and inherent constraints. The "how do they impact" part connects it directly to design concerns like speed of development, reliability, and user experience at scale.

- "How do we currently gather and utilize user data and analytics within our tech stack, and what opportunities exist to enhance our data-driven design capabilities?"

This focuses on the "how" of information flow crucial for design. Understanding how user behavior is tracked and analyzed is paramount for informed design decisions. It also opens a dialogue about improving data accessibility and tools for the design team, potentially leading to more personalized or adaptive user experiences.

- "What is our approach to platform extensibility and integration, both internally and with third-party services, and how does this affect our ability to create seamless and integrated user journeys?"

This "what" and "how" question addresses the interconnectedness of the tech stack. At the time of writing in june 2025, integration with other services (APIs, microservices, etc.) is vital. You need to know how easily new features or partnerships can be woven into the existing product without creating fragmented user experiences.

- "How do we manage our development lifecycle, from ideation to deployment, and what are the primary bottlenecks or challenges that currently impact the speed and quality of our feature delivery?"

This "how" question gets to the operational heart of the engineering team. You need to understand the design-to-development handoff, testing procedures, and deployment cadence. Identifying bottlenecks (e.g., slow testing, complex deployment) will help you advocate for process improvements that directly benefit the speed and quality of new design implementations.

"If you think good design is expensive,
you should look at the cost of bad design."
Dr. Ralf Speth

Chief Financial Officer (CFO)

The Chief Financial Officer's role in corporate strategy is long-term financial planning. The CFO ensures that the company has the resources to achieve its strategic objectives and that technology investments align with those goals while delivering a positive return on investment (ROI).[29]

A CFO's work involves raising capital, overseeing mergers and acquisitions, and assessing potential investment returns. They communicate with investors, lead financial discussions in quarterly board meetings, and create accurate financial models and forecasts to help the company anticipate future trends, identify potential economic risks, and make informed strategic decisions.

The CFO requires reliable financial data to justify ongoing investments such as hiring additional staff, purchasing equipment, and allocating travel budgets.

You can gain your CFO's support by being responsible for your team's budget. Demonstrating that you understand and care about the expenses your team incurs is essential for your credibility and influence in securing future resources. Financial literacy enables you to become an effective advocate for your team and a skilled negotiator, as you can translate the creative realm into business language.

If, like me, you did not learn to read financial statements during your education, you could take it upon yourself to understand which metrics are crucial for your company.

---

[29] Good, Cloud Doing. "CFOs and their role in technology decision making." *Cloud Doing Good*. Accessed April 29, 2025. https://www.cloudoingood.com/insights/cfos-and-their-role-in-technology-decision-making

Identifying which metrics are most critical to the CFO will help you and your team align with corporate strategy. Your CFO will appreciate your efforts to support their goals, whether to grow the bottom line or minimize the company's expenses. If you are meeting your CFO and your goal is to build rapport, you might start by asking these questions.

Questions for your CFO

- "What are the top three financial metrics you prioritize most for the company's overall success, and how does the design organization currently impact, or have the potential to impact, those metrics?"

  This question gets directly at the CFO's core financial priorities. Understanding these metrics (e.g., revenue growth, profit margin, customer acquisition cost, and lifetime value) allows you to align design initiatives with key business goals. Asking how design impacts them opens a dialogue about the value of design in financial terms.

- "How do we currently allocate our R&D and product development budgets, and what is the process for demonstrating ROI for these investments, especially those related to design-led initiatives?"

  This question uncovers the budgeting process and the CFO's expectations for demonstrating value. You need to understand how to make a case for design investments and how their success will be measured financially. It also reveals the company's comfort level with "qualitative" ROI metrics often associated with design.

- "What are our most significant cost drivers, both operationally and in product development, and how can the design team contribute to greater efficiency or cost optimization without compromising user experience or innovation?"

This shows you are thinking beyond just spending and considering how design can be a strategic partner in cost management. Design can impact costs through efficient workflows, reduced re-work, optimized resource utilization, and even by creating more intuitive products that reduce support costs.

- "How does the company view and measure customer lifetime value (CLTV), and what financial targets are we aiming for in terms of customer retention, expansion, and acquisition through product and design efforts?"

This connects design directly to customer value, which is a significant financial driver in tech. Understanding CLTV and associated targets helps you to focus design efforts on areas that will have the greatest long-term financial impact, such as improving retention through better user experience or driving expansion through new feature adoption.

- "What are the company's long-term financial growth strategies, including any plans for market expansion, new product categories, or M&A, and how can design play a proactive role in identifying and capitalizing on these opportunities?"

This question positions you as a strategic partner, not just an executor. It delves into the future financial trajectory of the company and invites a discussion on how design can be a foresight engine, helping to identify new markets, product opportunities, or even potential acquisition targets based on user needs and market trends.

To bridge the gap between theory and practice, we turn to executive Julie Baher. Drawing on her career at leading tech companies, she'll provide valuable insights into effectively aligning design and customer experience with the C-suite's strategic vision to drive tangible business outcomes.

EXECUTIVE INSIGHT WITH JULIE BAHER

Julie Baher is an experienced executive in the UX community and, at the time of writing, the Vice President of Customer Experience and Digital Strategy at Myriad Genetics. She has built a remarkable career by aligning her passions with her professional pursuits. With a diverse background spanning life sciences, enterprise, productivity tools, creative tools, and corporate websites, Julie has consistently led global teams to deliver impactful user experiences.

In our conversation, Julie emphasized the importance of finding companies where her values align with the organization's mission. She has excelled as an executive leader by working for companies that share her passion for innovation and user-centric design. Julie's journey inspires, demonstrating how a deep understanding of one's passions and values can lead to a fulfilling and successful career.

What led you to work in user experience design?

I've always been fascinated by the intersection of art and problem-solving. Even as a child, I remember thinking about how I could combine my love of math and creativity. It took me a while to figure out the exact path, but my early experiences in graphic design and software development solidified my interest in user-centered design. I'm drawn to the idea of creating functional and visually appealing solutions.

Once I discovered graphic design, I thought, "Why isn't this taught in schools?" It's applied art, not fine art. You're not trying to be a Rembrandt but creating practical, useful things. And I'm a practical person. I love designing posters and creating visual solutions.

That's why I kept combining my interests. I went to grad school to learn about the sciences so I could better design educational experiences. I was also drawn to software interface design. When I graduated, a friend suggested looking into user experience jobs. I had no idea what that was!

At the time, around 1999, not many roles existed in user experience design, but with the dot-com excitement, they were starting to grow. I joined a software start-up in Chicago, building an online MBA (remember Flash!). I then went to Xerox in Silicon Valley, California, and then Adobe, and it just kept going.

When did you transition from a research contributor to a managerial position?

About seven years into my career, my boss at Adobe invited me to become a manager. My response was, "I don't understand. What do you see in me?" It's ironic because now that I've been a manager for so long, I recognize it in my team members and invite them to manage. "You should be a manager. I'll get you an intern to practice."

It's fascinating that not everyone sees it in themselves. It's interesting how people can be so independent, and then be so surprised when their boss is like, 'You don't need me.'" So I can grow a team under them.

Surprisingly, I enjoy the interpersonal aspects of management. While some people prefer individual contributor roles, I find satisfaction in the opportunity to influence broader company initiatives. It's a bit cheesy, but it's true. As a manager, I can oversee multiple projects and make a more significant impact.

As a design leader, I'm interested in crafting the overall customer experience. But I'm particularly drawn to understanding how the company works. I want to know more about its operations and functions, and how I can influence them. My research background gives me a unique perspective on this.

As a kid, I loved Richard Scarry's book What Do People Do All Day? It gives you a peek into everyone's lives in the town, showing what's happening in every building, every room, and every street. I like knowing how things work and seeing the systems at play. That's what I appreciate about tackling an enormous scope—it opens doors for me in ways I never expected.

When did you become an executive leader?

That's a tricky question to answer. I feel like I'm fully embodying the role of vice president of design and UX in my current job and having a real voice at the table for the first time. In my previous director roles, there were moments when I embodied an executive leader. Still, I often felt limited by the perception of me as a team leader rather than a broader strategic thinker. I was leading initiatives, but not always at the scale I desired.

"I've learned to be more assertive about my role and avoid the common pitfalls of UX being overlooked or undervalued."

As vice president of design and customer experience at DNAnexus, I led a major product launch that felt like a huge accomplishment. However, due to the company's small size, there were limited opportunities for further growth. It was a one-time event, and we quickly returned to our smaller-scale projects.

I'm excited to have a more prominent leadership role at Myriad. It's been a shift in mindset, moving away from simply being the UX leader and toward positioning myself as a valuable strategic contributor. I've learned to be more assertive about my role and avoid the common pitfalls of UX being overlooked or undervalued.

I've been fortunate to work in life sciences, where there's a greater appreciation for the role of UX and a desire to have a great customer experience. Unlike some tech companies, they haven't developed the same exclusionary practices that often marginalize UX professionals. In tech companies, the product origin story frequently revolves around an engineer, perhaps with a business person, and UX is brought in later. You're never quite as core to the origin story or its current success. It's like, "Okay, yeah, the window dressing is lovely, but it has this awesome engine!"

Creating a product in life sciences requires many disciplines. It's a Venn diagram of software people, scientists, medical practitioners, bio-informaticists, marketers, and sometimes even hardware engineers, all working together.

It's more of a 'big tent' approach. We're not excluding anyone; it's more about recognizing that we already need a diverse range of disciplines to succeed. Having UX is a positive addition. It's like, "Yay, another team member!"

What do you believe sets you apart as an executive leader?

I most enjoy the problem-solving and strategic aspects of executive leadership. Collaborating with cross-functional teams to identify root causes, develop solutions, and implement effective strategies is particularly rewarding. A blend of design thinking and lean methodologies, like Six Sigma, can be a powerful approach to achieving these goals. Combining creativity and analytical rigor can drive innovation and continuous improvement.

Many people are skilled at operations but struggle with creative environments or ambiguous problems. I'm good at that—at figuring out how the organization works and how to actually get work done (at Citrix, I got an award for getting sh%& done).

How do you foster collaboration between product managers, designers, and engineers to ensure a cohesive product vision?

In my current role, I also lead the product management team. One essential part of product management is communicating across the business, which sets it apart from design. A junior product manager needs to talk to more people than a junior designer, who only needs to communicate with their immediate team.

Product managers must always explain their work to the business, talking to higher-level people, so I think a lot about how to mentor them on that. Often, someone might be great with their team but struggle to communicate strategically with the business. I try to help them understand that they need to be confident and present themselves as product experts when talking to directors and VPs. Product managers are the public face of what we build, so they need to be able to explain our products to the business.

This gives me more authority to comment on development work and other areas. I'm not just coming from UX, where you only talk about UI engineers. I'm involved in the entire stack, weighing in on decisions like using an outside firm for X to augment our development team or in discussions on business priorities.

Our designers are now more involved in these conversations because we are all one team. So, to foster collaboration, we work a lot on our design operations (I have a great leader running this) to make sure there is clear communication, quick handoffs, and thorough reviews with the product managers and engineers.

How do you leverage design thinking to drive innovation in complex environments?

A lot of our work feels like a Jenga tower. If you push on one thing, it can cause a domino effect elsewhere. That's why it's crucial to understand everything before we make changes. It's essentially workflow analysis and journey mapping. We have to take into account so many things: customer service, the billing department, our medical professionals, etc. So, thinking in terms of visual mapping is extremely helpful in showing the connections within the ecosystem, and we then base future concepts on that.

We are doing a lot of envisioning new journeys and then working backward on how to do the right projects to get us there.

How do you measure the success of your product in a competitive market, especially regarding user experience?

Since my team builds the tools that surround our products (the medical portals and patient tools), we get some metrics of user activity. However, the bigger picture of product success is captured better in the market research data, and then we have to tease out the portion that comes from our work.

I work closely with market research. They analyze our products and compare them to competitors across ten dimensions. Half of those were clinical-related, and I focused on the other half, which were experience-related. Things like how burdensome our product is for staff, how easy it is to order, and so on. We also look for feedback from our sales teams, who are on the front lines with our customers. We meet regularly with the commercial leadership to listen to their feedback and hear what they believe will move the needle on our product.

How do you ensure the UX metrics you track align with both business objectives and product goals?

I'm fortunate to have product management on my team, which helps align our work with clear business objectives. With two of the three key components (product, market, and technology) in place, it's easier to establish measurable metrics. I've been sharing a quarterly metric tracking report with these metrics, along with commentary on what they mean for the business. We track things like what channels our customers order on, which tools they use, conversion rates for our patient-driven test products, CSAT scores, etc.

Who do you collaborate with across departments, and how do you ensure effective teamwork and alignment on shared goals?

Working with cross-functional players is a daily part of my role. I have ongoing relationships with people like the SVP of Engineering Operations and the SVP of Revenue Cycle. My boss is the SVP of Product Management, and

I'm dotted-lined to our CTO. As a member of his staff, I meet with him regularly. I also frequently interact with the commercial team, which includes the Sales Vice Presidents, Business Unit Presidents, Sales Operations, and Area Sales Managers.

> *"I've realized that it's better to*
> *listen more and talk less."*

I have visibility into the plans for each of our business units, so I can align our team with their goals and make sure that our priority projects are what each business line needs. It's helpful to be part of the QBRs (quarterly business reviews) and close to our market research team that publishes studies about our products, our competitors' products, SWOT analyses, etc. All this helps me ensure the team understands the business needs and the 'why' behind them.

How have your interests influenced your career choices and helped you find passion in your work?

While the past 20 years of my career have been as a user experience leader, I've been fortunate to have worked in various industries. Wherever I worked, I could tell a story about how I connected personally to the company's mission. For example, I grew up doing darkroom photography, loved black-and-white prints, and worked in desktop publishing. So, Adobe allowed me to help creative professionals make fantastic art and designs. I had also worked in IT and built computers, so I found a connection at Citrix with our IT customers.

Later, I worked at Illumina, which develops DNA sequencing and array-based life sciences technologies to improve human health. I had been a biology undergrad and had always been interested in genetics, but I didn't want to be a lab researcher. So, I put that interest on the shelf. Then, at Illumina, I was able to help scientists by creating software and hardware for them to analyze genomic data.

Today, I work at Myriad, a genetic testing and precision medicine company that helps people understand their risk of developing diseases and how to treat them. I grew up as the daughter of a doctor, actually a fourth-generation MD. I'm the loser (kidding) who got a Ph.D., so while technically also "Dr. Baher," I'm not a medical doctor. Now, at Myriad, I'm helping doctors and patients find a path to better health through genetic insights. So, I love being able to put together my undergraduate degree in biology with my interest in medicine, my experiences building software, my interest in design, and my skills as a customer experience professional.

How do you manage stress and maintain a healthy work-life balance?

Sometimes, I find that work issues are rattling around in my head. While I try not to work on the weekend, thinking about things over and over again is annoying. So, I've learned to get it out of my head by writing it down—by putting words to the problems and the feelings, I can stop the endless ruminating.

I've become more aware of what pushes my buttons—some things don't bother me that bother other people, and vice versa. I try to put more words to things, acknowledge the feelings, and appropriately express them to others.

I've realized that it's better to listen more and talk less. My former boss told me that my neck turns red when I get angry or upset. That was a wake-up call. I realized that even though I think of myself as a calm person, my face still gets hot, I fidget, and my mind starts racing. So, I've been trying to sit with those feelings now while the other person is talking. I tell myself that I don't have to answer or respond immediately. So, granting myself some time to collect my thoughts and let my racing brain slow down has been very helpful.

I'm being more patient and measured before responding to people. I've been saying, "Tell me more" as a response more and more. I remind myself to hold the possibility that I've misunderstood or misinterpreted what they mean. This has helped a lot. When I say, "Tell me more," they often go into more detail, and I realize they were focused on something else, so I was ready to pounce after their first sentence. That's helped avoid negative situations. Plus, the other person feels more heard.

These are the things I've been focusing on to manage stress now that work is 100% remote for me: Taking purposeful breaks in the day—I try to take a lunch break and leave my office, sit somewhere else, eat, and read my personal emails or the news. The rest of the day, I only focus on work, so I don't mix personal time with work hours.

I'm trying to take more time to reflect on challenging things. I'm fairly impatient and want to solve things quickly, but I've learned that it's okay to take a little time to work through stressful or emotional issues at work. I also do the same for others. If it's a difficult topic, I'll say, "Think about this over the weekend," or "We can regroup on this next week; you don't have to have an answer now." Other than that, continuing to exercise and maintain good physical health helps!

CHAPTER 5

Your Role in Business Strategy: Decoding Business

STRATEGY FOR DESIGN LEADERS

Quantifying UX Without Crushing Creativity

Yes, quantifiable business metrics give tech companies valuable insights to hit their targets. However, leaning too heavily on this hard data to gauge the impact of user experience design can actually smother creativity and innovation. Trying to deliver design solutions that only serve the company's strategic objectives often feels like fighting on someone else's turf, using business metrics that aren't inherently yours.

A holistic approach that marries quantitative data with qualitative insights helps you understand the nuanced aspects of human behavior and the emotional power of design, truly to show its worth to both users and the business. As Ryan Scott, founder of Accelerate Design, wisely states, "Metrics measure changes in human behavior, and design connects to profits through understanding user experience."

In your role as a design leader in tech, you're always walking a tightrope: on one side, meeting the business strategy on its own terms, and on the other, fulfilling your vision as the creative head for the company's design direction. This chapter dives deep into the realm of hard, quantitative metrics—a facet I admittedly came to understand later in my career. To truly excel as a design executive, you need to create product experiences that demonstrably grow the business. This journey starts with a crystal-clear understanding of your company's business strategy. Put simply, you'll thrive by being an integral part of the solution in answering the three core questions every business needs to master:

1. Who are our target customers?

2. What makes our product uniquely valuable?

3. How do we solve customer problems better than the competition?

1. WHO ARE OUR TARGET CUSTOMERS?

Businesses often start with a broad idea of their target audience, but they need to dig deeper to be sure that what they build will target customers who want to and actually will buy it. Tech companies will invest in research to discover who to target and what those customer segments value about the product or service. For example, one of Netflix's target audiences is millennials. They spend more time on their devices than watching TV and value convenience, quality content, and a personalized viewing experience. Knowing this makes it much easier to decide what product and service to offer them.

As an executive, you have access to customers in ways that were impossible before your promotion to this role. For example, you can learn what the customer support team is hearing about customer pain points and gain insider insights into customer problems from top salespeople. If you want to test a hypothesis, you can ask your data science or market research team. Understanding your target customers gives you a wealth of creative ideas to share with your team to work with.

2. WHAT MAKES OUR PRODUCT UNIQUELY VALUABLE?

A critical aspect of your strategic leadership lies in deeply internalizing and articulating the product's unique value proposition. This understanding is the bedrock upon which impactful design vision is built. By grasping what truly differentiates your products, you can leverage design to directly amplify that uniqueness, ensuring it resonates powerfully with users and the market. This strategic alignment of design and core product value can be achieved through four key design-centric approaches, which we will now recap.

"Design is the last great competitive advantage."
Seth Godin

Deeply Understand and Solve User Problems

To deeply understand and solve user problems, their pain points, and unmet needs, you'll want to champion a diverse research toolkit, much like we did at Yahoo and the online news site redesign. This could include deep dives into user behavior through ethnographic research, visualizing their end-to-end interactions with journey mapping, understanding their emotional landscape with empathy mapping, and fixing customer pain points.

Consider Sam Farbo, an American industrial designer who transformed kitchen utensil design with the Swivel Peeler. His ability to empathize with his wife's struggle to alleviate her arthritis pain while peeling potatoes and identify a practical solution resulted in the iconic OXO Good Grips peeler. The peeler is celebrated for its innovative design, accessibility, and user-friendliness and has maintained a 4.8-star rating on Amazon for nearly three decades. Its inclusion in MoMA's permanent collection and recognition with the Fast Company Timeless Design award highlights its lasting impact.

Once you have a rich understanding of your users and their pain points, transform them into opportunities by asking "How might we" questions. For instance, "How might we stop customers from not completing an online purchase because of unexpected costs at checkout (especially shipping)?"

Studying user needs continuously helps address current and future needs. For instance, the OXO brand was created by standardizing the handle design of their potato peeler for use across various kitchen utensils more cost-effectively. Today, OXO is one of several brands owned by Helen of Troy in the Home & Outdoor segment, which contributes 39% of sales, generating annual revenues of $2.22 billion and an operating profit of $272.6 million. By addressing the challenge of peeling potatoes for his wife, Sam established a business that anticipated the needs of a much broader audience.

Craft a Distinct and Desirable User Experience

Define a Unique Product Personality

Infuse your product with a distinct brand voice and style that resonates with the target audience and sets it apart from competitors to create an emotional connection and build brand loyalty.

Ask Your Team

- What kind of 'relationship' do we want users to have with our product? Do we want them to see it as a trusted assistant, a quirky companion, a powerful tool, or something else entirely? (Encourages thinking about the long-term user-product bond.)

- How does our product's personality differentiate us from competitors in a meaningful way? What makes our personality uniquely 'ours' in the market?" (Encourages differentiation beyond features, focusing on emotional connection.)

- What is the single most important feeling we want users to have when interacting with our product? (Focuses on emotional impact, which is central to personality.)

Design for Delight

Beyond usability, how might you incorporate moments of surprise, joy, and delight throughout the user journey? These memorable interactions can create strong positive associations with the product.

Ask Your Team

- Where are the unexpected moments or 'micro-interactions' in the user journey where we can introduce a small, delightful surprise that goes above and beyond expectation?

Ensure Seamless and Consistent Experiences

Creating a cohesive and intuitive experience across all touchpoints (web, mobile, physical products, etc.) will prevent friction, reduce development and customer care costs, and build user confidence.

Ask Your Team

- How are we identifying and addressing inconsistencies across the entire user journey?

- How do we measure and track our user experience consistency?

- What are our key metrics for identifying friction points or inconsistencies in the user journey?

DRIVE INNOVATION AND DIFFERENTIATION

Explore Emerging Technologies

Support your teams in educating themselves on emerging technologies to help innovate both the user and product experience and expand their toolset.

Ask Your Team

- What emerging technologies are you most excited about, and why do you believe they hold significant potential to address unmet user needs or create entirely new user experiences?

- If we were to experiment with [emerging technology], what are some proof-of-concept experiments we could run that would quickly validate its value proposition for our users and inform our long-term strategy?

- What ethical considerations, potential biases, or negative user impacts do we need to be acutely aware of if we integrate [emerging technology] into our products? How can we design proactively to mitigate these risks?

Challenge Conventions

Don't be afraid to question established design patterns and explore unconventional solutions that can lead to breakthrough innovations.

Ask Your Team

- What widely accepted 'truths' or 'best practices' in our industry or product category are we inadvertently adhering to, and what would happen if we challenged them completely?

- What's the riskiest idea we've shelved because it felt 'too out there'? How might we prototype and test a low-cost version of it to truly understand its potential or pitfalls?

Foster a Culture of Experimentation

Encourage your team to rapidly explore new ideas, prototype, test, and learn from failures. This iterative approach can lead to uniquely valuable product features.

Ask Your Team

- What problem are we trying to solve with this idea/ design, and what is our clear hypothesis about how this experiment will address that problem?

- How will we measure the success (or failure) of this experiment, and what specific data points will tell us if our hypothesis was valid?

- How can we share our experimental findings more broadly with the wider product and engineering teams, and even the organization?

BUILD A STRONG DESIGN SYSTEM AND BRAND LANGUAGE

Create a Scalable and Consistent Design System

A well-defined design system ensures visual and interaction consistency across the product, improving efficiency, saving time to market, enabling rapid scaling, and reducing development costs.

Ask Your Team

- What are the core problems our current design and development processes face that a design system is uniquely positioned to solve?" (e.g., inconsistency, slow delivery, technical debt, communication silos)

- What are the design principles that will underpin this system, ensuring it reflects our brand identity and user experience goals?

- What processes will we put in place for contributing new components, requesting changes, and deprecating outdated elements?

- What tools and technologies are essential for building, documenting, and distributing our design system effectively?

Develop a Clear and Compelling Brand Language

Ensure that the product's visual and verbal elements communicate the brand's unique value proposition effectively and consistently across all surfaces.

Ask Your Team

- How does our proposed brand language (visual, verbal, and experiential) directly embody our core company values and mission?

- What is our process for ensuring the brand language is authentic and resonates with our diverse user base?

- How will we gather ongoing feedback to evolve it effectively over time?

- How will our brand language scale across all current and future touchpoints, from product UI, marketing campaigns, and social media to customer service interactions and physical experiences?

3. HOW DO WE SOLVE CUSTOMER PROBLEMS BETTER THAN THE COMPETITION?

Solving customer problems more effectively than the competition hinges on a robust product-market fit strategy. This strategy is built upon three core pillars: capitalizing on technical advancements and market inflection points, identifying and exploiting design gaps, and meticulously optimizing existing products and services for competitive superiority. The following explanations and examples illustrate how design has been successfully leveraged at other tech companies to solve customer problems better than the competition.

Capitalizing on Inflection Points and Technological Advancements

Capitalizing on inflection points and technological advancements involves strategically identifying and seizing pivotal moments of technological or societal change to create new product experiences or significantly enhance existing ones, thereby leapfrogging the competition. These inflection points can emerge from groundbreaking technological innovations, such as the arrival of the internet, the mobile revolution, the advent of advanced AI, or the development of novel materials, which can initiate entirely new markets or fundamentally transform existing ones. A prime example of how technological advancement has opened up a new range of product possibilities is ride-sharing applications like Lyft and Uber. These businesses could not have existed before the introduction of the Apple iPhone 4S, which incorporated a built-in GPS locator, enabling riders and drivers to be algorithmically connected for the first time in history.

Companies that understand and creatively apply these technologies, like Apple did with the smartphone, gain a decisive advantage. Similarly, significant shifts in how users live, work, communicate, or consume information, as Netflix masterfully leveraged with the rise of streaming, present fertile ground for innovative product and service design.

As Intuit has demonstrated, even regulatory changes can serve as inflection points, creating opportunities for design-led solutions that meet new compliance needs. Additionally, market disruptions, often driven by innovative business models or unexpected competitors, require a design-centric approach to adaptation and innovation. This ensures relevance and ongoing competitiveness, much like traditional automakers navigating the transition to electric vehicles. As a creative leader, you stay attuned to these shifts, envision the design possibilities they unlock, champion agile experimentation, and advocate for the necessary investment to bring these forward-thinking experiences to life.

Identifying and Exploiting Design and Gaps

This requires understanding the existing competitive landscape to pinpoint unmet user needs or areas where current solutions lack usability, desirability, or overall value. By strategically innovating in these 'design gaps,' you can create products and services that resonate more deeply with customers and offer a superior experience. Zoom is an excellent example of a pattern-breaking tech company establishing a new product-market fit through groundbreaking market innovation.

In 2011, when Zoom was founded, video conferencing was often clunky, unreliable, and costly. Technical glitches, poor audio and video quality, and complicated user interfaces frequently hindered available options. The team at Zoom, led by Eric S. Yuan, recognized the increasing demand for seamless and accessible video communication, particularly as remote work and global collaboration became more prevalent.[30] The breakthrough innovation involved developing a platform prioritizing simplicity, reliability, and high-quality video and audio. Their technology was built from the ground up to optimize low bandwidth and handle large meetings with minimal latency. The team emphasized user experience, creating an intuitive interface that made it easy for

---

[30] "Here's How Zoom Provides Industry-Leading Video Capacity." *Zoom*. September 29, 2022. Accessed April 30, 2025. https://www.zoom.com/en/blog/zoom-can-provide-increase-industry-leading-video-capacity/

anyone to join or host a meeting. As a result, Zoom established a new product-market fit by effectively democratizing video conferencing, making it more accessible than ever to a broader audience with its user-friendly interface and reliability.

After its launch, Zoom quickly gained traction among businesses and educational institutions. The pandemic accelerated Zoom's growth, but its innovative foundation had already created a solid product-market fit, including a freemium model that enhanced accessibility. Zoom did not merely improve existing video conferencing technology; it fundamentally transformed how people communicate remotely, disrupting competing products like Microsoft Teams, Google Meet, Cisco Webex, GoToMeeting, and Slack. It set a new benchmark for video communication by prioritizing ease of use and reliability. Zoom's valuation has reached $26.75 billion, and revenue is projected to hit $4.5 billion by 2025, proving once again that good design is good business.

Meticulously Optimizing Existing Products and Services

This involves a continuous and data-driven approach to refining your current offerings. By rigorously analyzing user feedback, market trends, and competitive weaknesses, you can iteratively enhance your products and services to outperform the competition in features, performance, user experience, and overall value proposition. This ongoing optimization ensures you maintain a competitive edge and continuously address customer problems more effectively. At Asana, Anshuman Kumar led the meticulous optimization of the existing products and services, resulting in millions of dollars of annual recurring revenue for the company. Read about how he achieved this in my interview.

EXECUTIVE INSIGHT WITH ANSHUMAN KUMAR

Anshuman Kumar leads an international team of over 100 product designers, brand designers, design operations specialists, design systems specialists, and content designers. Before Asana, he was a senior staff manager at Google, designing the foundation for augmented and virtual reality products. Before Google, he worked as a lead interaction designer for Yahoo, crafting the next generation of editorial, advertiser, and publisher experiences and content. Anshuman grew up in India, receiving a degree in architecture from Dr. A.P.J. Abdul Kalam Technical University and a master's in interaction design from the prestigious Institute of Technology in Bombay.

Tell us about your journey to becoming SVP and Head of Design at Asana.

I grew up thinking that the word leader only applied to political leaders, so I never thought I'd be one. I had not imagined that leadership could also be a profession. Growing up in India, one of my favorite books was The Geography of Thought: How Asians and Westerners Think Differently...and Why by Richard E. Nisbett, which I read in my early 20s in college.

The book portrays Western society as individualistic: You represent yourself and will fight for your rights. The eastern part of the world is very community-oriented. If someone tries to stand out, they are frowned upon. You're supposed to be a part of the community. That book gave me a framework for how I think.

I didn't pursue leadership roles, though they were somewhere in the back of my mind. I didn't want or expect to become a leader; I just wanted to make things, build things, and do things. I knew I was empathetic and patient with people, and I took care to handle and address situations. My leadership journey has resulted from people believing I can be a leader, and people have given me a shot, a stretch opportunity. They thought I could do more than my current role. This has happened multiple times in my career. Even now, I didn't join as the head of design at Asana three years ago. I joined as a senior director for one business division, and then opportunities presented themselves, until eventually I was asked to lead the entire team.

How long have you worked in the tech industry, and how long before you were tapped for management?

I've been in tech for 16 years and got into management at the end of my 5th year when my then-manager asked me, "Hey, would you like to lead a team and manage them? I asked, "Why do you feel I should manage a team?" He said, "Oh, I think you'll be a good manager." He saw something in me, and I decided to take the opportunity. Stepping into management was tricky and very uncomfortable at first. My first team consisted of people who were my peers, and I used to go and have lunch with everyone. Overnight, I was their manager, and the next day, when we had lunch, they would be like, "Is this you, or are you my manager?"

"My leadership journey has resulted from people believing I can be a leader, and people have given me a shot."

How do you distinguish between managing and executive leadership?

Management is a form of leadership. You don't need to manage to be a leader. I have design leaders on my team. They're phenomenal leaders. They don't manage people, but they manage the work and shape strategy. I don't think people management is necessary to be a leader, but it might be required if you are looking for a specific position in a company.

As an executive leader, the buck stops with me for design at Asana, and that's a very different sense of responsibility from leading a part of the organization. It has some weight. I'm balancing and harmonizing multiple force vectors from our business needs to product direction. From the people on my team to my cross-functional partners, the altitude at which I am balancing these force vectors has changed. The challenge is that I must play those force vectors out and imagine how they will affect the frontline designer or manager. Then, I reverse calculate and see how I adjust these force vectors through my actions and words. That's the tricky part, but it's also the fun part.

What do you enjoy about the unique aspects of executive design work?

I love living in the future and assuming different scenarios. It's fun to think, if we did X, that would lead to Y. I'm creative and enjoy scenario planning, where I run those situations through a design process mentally. I also enjoy seeing people on my team succeed, doing their work, and knowing it's the best part of their professional careers. It's very fulfilling in a very indirect way.

What makes creating organizations rewarding as a design executive?

As an executive, I'm leveraging a design process to help inform a plan, the outcome of which is not pixels but decisions. Creating an organization is very similar to solving a design problem. I am running scenario planning through a design process, asking open-ended questions. "Do I know enough about the people involved in the situation? What are their hopes and desires in this situation? With this insight, what three or four things could I do with the organization?"

Next, I talk with the stakeholders to gauge their reactions to these ideas. This is where designers play a critical role in organizational development, whether creating a vision for the design team or a product strategy aligned with the business. I understand all the focus areas and responsibilities and surround them with a structured design process.

What has informed your design process over time?

When I started my tech career, the design processes that existed then were built for a different pace of product development. When I began my career with Yahoo, projects were not running on a two-week sprint. Branch cuts (when the codebase is isolated and prepared for release while allowing development to continue) didn't happen every week. In college, in 2005, the design process felt almost like it was for industrial design. You're building a chair; you have one chance to make it, and then it's out in the world for sale. You can't iterate on that in real time.

The pace and interactiveness of today's product development processes have challenged human-centered design. The core remains the same: You need to understand your customer. You need to develop solutions, validate them, explore and expand on them, and test them before going to production. Recently, the weight and amount of time teams spend working on designs have changed in the design process, which has shifted because of their iterative nature.

Today, it's simpler to take a more significant risk. It's like launching something, getting feedback, and iterating. The fact that we can do that is both empowering and limiting.

It is empowering because it allows you to correct mistakes. However, it is also limited because teams and companies generally don't want to spend time making things perfect. It's about shipping things fast, learning, iterating, forming, and shaping the product based on user signals. The more it becomes real-time, the more the process weights will shift.

The human-centered design process still works, but the weight we assign to different stages has shifted drastically. With AI, it will shift even further.

"The most unique change about being a design executive is that I live far into the future."

What are the primary challenges you face as an executive design leader compared to a design manager?

The most surface-level change is that as an executive, I'm a little further away from execution than I was as a design manager at Google.

As I have delved a few levels deeper, my responsibilities and accountability have expanded. As SVP at Asana, I am responsible for a multi-million-dollar budget. I have to figure out how to spend that money on, for example, design teams and talent acquisition, design tools and technology, research and user experience studies, design strategy and innovation, brand development and consistency, as well as design collaboration and partnerships.

The most unique change about being a design executive is that I live far into the future. As a design manager at Google, I lived six months to one year in the future; today, my time dimension is about three years. So, I'm building a sustainable team that will thrive for the next three years.

What design activities have you needed to prioritize more since transitioning from a design manager to an executive role?

As a design manager, people expected me to be looking at their Figma files to see pixel-level design work. As SVP, I was told I needed to stop going into people's files because when designers saw my avatar or mouse pointer moving in their files, they were concerned I would judge or evaluate their work. Today, if I have to look at someone's work, I don't go into Figma unannounced, and I drop them a comment to encourage them before I leave.

How can design leaders effectively communicate with executive peers to demonstrate an understanding of business goals and values?

I was fortunate to start my design career working on ad products at Yahoo. It was amazing because it helped me understand the business of the web. I worked on ad products for search display and search advertising, building tools for both the buyer and seller sides and designing new ad formats.

Surfaces are the visible parts of a product that a customer can touch, feel, and see. Ad formats are very, very sensitive surfaces. Changing the font size to a point bigger has an impact. Changing the type and color also has an effect. Adding more spacing around a button also has an impact.

It was a phenomenal experience for a new designer to understand the web business and learn that every pixel you light up can impact revenue.

Today, again, I am fortunate to work on a product in the software as a service (SaaS) industry. Asana is in the work management vertical of SaaS and competes in a crowded product space. The more competition exists, the more product design becomes a critical differentiator. I'm fortunate to work in a competitive business market where ease of use is essential to business because it becomes a differentiator when you sell a product. I'm also fortunate that Asana understands the value of design as a differentiator and empowers the design team with the responsibility of how much we follow through on that expectation.

At one point, the business set annual recurring revenue (ARR) as a North Star for some of the R&D teams, including design. This led to much optimization work, where we could make small changes and see a direct impact on revenue. Choosing what to optimize took a lot of work. At that moment, my team and I saw a force vector in a particular direction. It was not ideal for a design team when a dollar number evaluates everything, but we thought about how to use this direction and turn it in favor of the design team and the overall product.

So, we launched an initiative in which the design team audited multiple critical surfaces where we felt revenue-generating possibilities existed. We identified every possible UX bug and documented it. We asked the cross-functional teams, "Hey, before you shoot in the dark, here is a list of things we believe can help drive revenue. We have already documented them and supplied some solutions; please pick what to optimize from this list." People started picking from the list because we did 30% of the work.

We also created a leaderboard to track the number of experiments conducted by teams and their impact on AI. It became a game, motivating teams to compete. Teams then focused on improving the quality of their experiments and the overall product. The leaderboard became a tool the design team could be proud of because it drove positive product improvements.

My role as a leader in this situation was to identify false trade-offs. When business needs and design goals seem to conflict, it's the leader's job to avoid making hasty compromises that might harm either side. I had to find solutions that satisfied both the business's requirements and the design team's vision. This involved reframing the problem and looking at the situation from different angles to identify areas of common ground, prioritizing goals, finding ways to balance them, and encouraging open communication and collaboration between business and design teams to find mutually beneficial solutions.

By effectively navigating these challenges, we created a positive and productive work environment where the business goals of ARR and the design team's goal of a better product experience were valued.

I actively drove the work and gradually let go as the teams built enough momentum to identify the issues within their surfaces. Most of the time, they already knew the bugs were backlogged as a P2 (the task affects customers). Still, there is a non-technical workaround, or P3 (the task doesn't affect customers), but until we had the list and the leaderboard, they needed more time to prioritize fixing them.

What started as a moment to improve the quality of the product in addition to driving ARR later became a cultural shift across the R&D team, where everyone began to believe that the quality of experience and the details are as important as the features themselves. This self-realization that the team had was the biggest win for me.

What strategies did you use to convince the executive team of the importance of this prioritization framework?

I went to the chief product officer and said, "We're going to make $12 million in six months." Who would say no to that?

This is where I feel the future of design belongs. It's not the most glorious, creative future, but the design should start owning P&L (profit and loss) to measure the financial outcome of an investment or trade over time. No one is going to give P&L to design leaders. We have to say, "Hey, I'm just going to do it. I will set up very ambitious targets, which I will likely miss, but I will pursue them." And if you keep hitting the target over time, things change, and goals become achievable.

What led you to achieve $12 million ARR through design optimization?

I selectively and strategically showed my manager examples from research of product problems affecting the user experience on the payments and new user adoption surfaces. I intentionally picked ones affecting user adoption, retention, and churn; there were 50 more. I asked, "Can we all agree that these are essential things to improve our product and make $12m in six months?" The answer was yes! We made $10 million in annual recurring revenue that year.

How are you informed about the latest design trends and technologies?

I don't stay updated on design trends, and in some ways, I don't care about them too much. However, I have been involved in two big technology trends that have come and gone: VR and AR. I was on the founding teams of both those efforts at Google. Over time, I have observed technical and design trends with curiosity but only a little anchorage.

When I look to the future, I see how people are changing. For example, Asana is a work management company that helps teams succeed, coordinate better, be clearer, and have a single source of truth. As an executive design leader looking ahead, I see three tectonic shifts happening right now.

The first is generational. Gen Z has a very different work-focused mindset, and its values work differently.[31] They will make up over 30% of the workforce by 2030. That is not a trend; it's happening at a slow pace. It's happening in an invisible way all around us, and we can't see or observe it yet.

---

[31] Generation Z in the Workplace by Ang Richard

The second is technological. AI is more than a trend because people see enough value in it. I am dyslexic, so in many ways, ChatGPT has become my co-writer about anything that I want to write. I have set up bots based on my writing style preferences to leverage when talking to my team and others. AI is going to be here. It's going to change how people work, operate, and create.

The third shift in the workspace is around the workspace and teams working remotely. It's a remnant of the pandemic, but it will stay in some shape or form. But when I look three years ahead, I'm trying to forecast how these three things combine and what it means to our product. If I can develop a perspective, share it with others, and see the gaps in my thinking, I can picture it three years from now. Then, the moment I start feeling confident about that picture, I begin considering our daily decisions.

For example, the design organization at Asana. When I joined, there was a disproportionate number of L5s with 7 to 8 years of expertise and leadership experience—often called principals.

Asana needed good system thinkers with good visual design and craft skills when they were hired. Looking ahead, I see these senior people want to grow to L6 and L7. We will have space for some, but not all, to grow. Once I started imagining this outcome, I realized it was not sustainable because it would mean a lot of pressure at that time, there would be a lot of attrition, and having the most senior designers on the team would not be a good thing for morale.

So, over the last year, I've allowed any L5 and L6 attrition to happen and started an early career program where we started to hire L3s whose work focuses on prototyping and modeling to develop solutions to design briefs. Today, we have 4 times more early-career designers than we had one year back. By coming from a place of living in the future three years from now, these L3s and L4s that we have hired today will become the design leaders for the organization.

Diversity was a significant factor, and bringing in early-career designers and letting them become tomorrow's leaders supports diversity better than playing musical chairs with existing design leaders and poaching them from other companies. This is an example of the future state I want the design team to be in two to three years and the actions I can take today.

CHAPTER 6

Quantifying Product Design

KEY METRICS FOR UX DESIGN EXECUTIVES

I vividly remember my first board meeting, where I was struck by the board members' effortless grasp of financial data. As the quarterly reports were shared around the table, all eyes—and bespoke eyewear—were fixed on the spreadsheets in front of them. Their ability to comprehend the company's financial health, identify key trends, and propose strategic recommendations took seconds. I watched in awe; the only thing I could compare it to was how one thinks during a design review. Now that I was working with board members for the sake of my team, I needed to understand how to leverage quantitative as well as qualitative metrics and connect the impact of our work directly to the business bottom line.

Inspired by the financial expertise of the board members, I embarked on improving my business knowledge and connecting product design outcomes to business metrics. You probably already understand what all these tech business metrics mean and how they relate to user experience design. But if you'd like a refresher, here is a list of typical financial metrics used in tech companies, with my suggestions and examples of how you could align with and deliver on them.

Average Order Value (AOV)

Average Order Value measures the average amount a customer spends per transaction. A higher AOV correlates with increased revenue and indicates that customers purchase more frequently and spend more per transaction, leading to greater customer satisfaction and a willingness to invest more in the brand. AOV helps marketers identify opportunities to bundle products, offer upsells, or create premium offerings as part of their product strategy to boost overall revenue.

It's not my place to tell you how to design for a retail experience, however, if you're focused on improving AOV it helps to understand how the data is tracked so you can align on its usage, tracking, reporting, and provide feedback on product recommendations, allowing the system to continuously improve and AOV keeps growing.

Some companies offer tools and platforms that enable businesses to track and analyze AOV. Analytics platforms for web and apps, such as Google Analytics, Adobe Analytics, Amplitude, and Piwik PRO, monitor and assess AOV, providing insights into customer behavior and sales performance. E-commerce platforms like Shopify and Squarespace feature dashboards that display AOV. Customer relationship management (CRM) systems integrate with e-commerce platforms and analytics tools to provide a comprehensive view of customer data, including purchase history and AOV.

Ask Yourself

- To increase Average Order Value, what design-led initiatives do you believe hold the most potential to encourage customers to discover and adopt higher-value offerings, increase their basket size, or engage with premium features directly?

AOV Resources

- Sherwin, Katie. "UX Guidelines for Ecommerce Product Pages." *NN/g.* November 24, 2019. Accessed April 30, 2025. www.nngroup.com/articles/ecommerce-product-pages/

- Dopson, Elise. "13 Checkout Optimization Tips To Increase Ecommerce Revenue (2024)." *Shopify UK.* Accessed April 30, 2025. www.shopify.com/uk/blog/checkout-process-optimization

- Wallace, Lauren. "Average Order Value: 10 Practical Ways to Increase Cart Size." Salesforce. June 6, 2024. Accessed April 30, 2025. www.salesforce.com/blog/average-order-value

Average Revenue Per User (ARPU)

Average Revenue Per User measures the average revenue generated by each user over a specific period. By analyzing ARPU, businesses can make informed decisions about pricing, promotions, and monetization strategies and compare their performance to industry standards and competitors. For instance, if a company generates $500,000 in revenue in a month and has 10,000 active users, the ARPU would be:

$$\text{ARPU} = \$500,000 \ / \ 10,000 \text{ users} = \$50 \text{ per user}$$

For example, Netflix boosts ARPU by analyzing user viewing histories and preferences while tailoring its content suggestions, resulting in higher user satisfaction and longer watch times. Duolingo, a language learning app, motivates users to practice regularly through engaging user interfaces and gamification tools such as XP points, streaks, and leaderboards. Its premium subscription model offers ad-free learning, unlimited training, and offline access, enhancing user value and generating revenue. Design teams drove the success of both Duolingo and Netflix in increasing ARPU.

Ask Yourself

- What could we design that would clearly demonstrate and communicate the value of our premium features or higher tiers and motivate users to upgrade or subscribe?"

ARPU Resource

- Farley, Ryan. "ARPU: How to Calculate and Interpret Average Revenue Per User." April 28, 2023. Accessed April 30, 2025. https://blog.hubspot.com/service/arpu

Average Time Spent (ATS)

Average Time Spent helps businesses evaluate user engagement and satisfaction. Users who spend more time with a product are more likely to feel satisfied and loyal, providing the company with opportunities to explore additional revenue streams such as upselling, cross-selling, advertisements, or subscriptions. In contrast, a low ATS may indicate usability issues, a lack of engaging content, or a disconnect between user expectations and the product's value proposition, all of which can contribute to churn. Businesses that maximize the time customers spend on their platforms include short-form video platforms like TikTok, video sites like YouTube, messaging and gaming applications, and streaming services like Disney+ and Hulu.

ATS data helps you, as a design leader, understand how users interact with the product. It can help create a complete user journey map when combined with other customer insights and data. A product with higher user engagement can stand out in a crowded market, and a product experience that keeps users engaged can be a significant differentiator.

Ask Yourself

- How are we identifying and addressing moments of user friction, confusion, or boredom that might lead to early exit, and what design interventions can turn these into opportunities for deeper engagement?"

ATS Resource

- "Average Time on Page: Proven Strategies for Site Optimization." Accessed April 30, 2025. https://contentsquare.com/blog/average-time-on-page/

- Kemp, Simon. "The time we spend on social media — DataReportal – Global Digital Insights." January 31, 2024. Accessed April 30, 2025. https://datareportal.com/reports/digital-2024-deep-dive-the-time-we-spend-on-social-media/

Churn Rate

When a customer stops using a product or service over a specific period, it directly impacts revenue and growth, called churn.

Churn Rate = (Number of Customers Lost / Number of Total Customers at the Start of the Period) x 100

There's no universally "good" or "bad" churn rate threshold, as it varies greatly depending on the industry, business model, and company stage. However, there are some general guidelines and factors to consider. For SaaS companies like Zoom, a "good" churn rate is often between 3% and 5% monthly, but this can differ. Enterprise SaaS, like SAP, may target an even lower monthly rate, around 1% to 2%. Anything above 5% monthly is generally regarded as a cause for concern. Subscription-based businesses, like Spotify, are susceptible to churn, with consumer subscription services exhibiting higher churn, particularly for non-essential services, experiencing 10% or more monthly. Imagine if you led the design of a subscription-based streaming service, and the business objective was to reduce churn by 50%.

Ask Yourself

- How can user behavior analytics and qualitative research identify the moments of friction, confusion, or unmet value in the user journey that directly lead to churn?

Churn Resource

- Kumar, Haris. "What Is Ecommerce Churn Rate & How To Calculate It?." June 20, 2024. Accessed April 30, 2025. https://www.chargebee.com/blog/ecommerce-churn-rate/

- "Subscription churn basics: What businesses need to know." Stripe. January 23, 2024. Accessed April 30, 2025. https://stripe.com/gb/resources/more/subscription-churn-101

Click-through Rate (CTR)

Click-through rate gauges how frequently users interact with ads from online advertising campaigns, email marketing, and website content. A higher CTR is preferable to a lower one because it signifies that the user finds the ad relevant, leading to increased traffic, enhanced brand visibility, and improved conversion rates. The formula is the number of clicks divided by the number of impressions multiplied by 100. Therefore, if your ad appears in search results 1,000 times (impressions) and receives 50 clicks, your CTR would be 5%.

Design can improve CTR by emphasizing a clear visual hierarchy, concise messaging, and engaging visuals. You can enhance the user experience by ensuring all ads function seamlessly across all platforms, particularly on mobile. Landing pages—the pages users see after clicking an ad—must be relevant, load quickly, and provide a clear path for users to follow. A/B testing is an effective method to compare different design elements and determine what works best. Elements of persuasive design, such as using colors to evoke emotions and create desired responses, offering social proof through customer testimonials, fostering a sense of urgency with limited-time offers, and ensuring contextual relevance, all drive a substantial CTR. Different platforms have varying ad formats, so understanding different ad formats can enhance engagement.

Ask Yourself

- What are the top 3-5 user journeys with the lowest CTRs? What hypotheses does the team have about the underlying design-related friction points or unmet expectations preventing clicks in those specific scenarios?"

CTR Resource

- Bohan, Donna-Marie. "How To Increase Average CTR." January 3, 2024. Accessed April 30, 2025. https://www.bloomreach.com/en/blog/how-to-increase-average-click-through-rate

- Storm, Macy. "What's a Good Click-through Rate (CTR) for Your Industry?" Accessed April 30, 2025. https://www.webfx.com/blog/marketing/whats-good-click-rate-ctr-industry/

Conversion Rates

Conversion rates measure the percentage of website visitors who complete a desired action, such as purchasing, signing up for a newsletter, or downloading an app. A high conversion rate indicates that the product's design effectively guides users toward the intended action. Conversely, a low conversion rate suggests that UX design issues may prevent users from completing the desired action, the content is irrelevant, or it fails to meet their expectations.

Businesses prioritize conversion rates because they directly affect revenue. For instance, if 100 people visit a website and 10 make purchases, the conversion rate is 10%. Spotify is known for its strong conversion rates, transitioning users from free ad-supported music and podcasts to its Premium service; this is essential for the company, as paid subscribers account for 90% of their revenue. UX design can enhance a strong conversion growth rate (CGR) by incorporating a prominent and compelling call to action (CTA) that motivates users to take the desired action. Creating a user-friendly interface that aligns with the brand, is easy to navigate, and loads quickly is critical. Mobile optimization ensures the product is designed for smartphone users. Moreover, trust and credibility are built through secure payment options, positive reviews, and a strong brand presence across all channel surfaces.

Ask Yourself

- What experimental design approaches hold the most untapped potential for significantly improving conversion rates?

Conversation Rate Resource

- "23 Essential Spotify Statistics You Need to Know in 2023." Accessed April 30, 2025. https://thesocialshepherd.com/blog/spotify-statistics

Customer Acquisition Cost (CAC)

Customer acquisition cost measures the average expense associated with acquiring a new customer for a business. A lower CAC indicates that a business acquires customers efficiently and is calculated by dividing the acquisition costs by the number of new customers. So, if a company spends $12,000 on a marketing campaign that results in 100 new customers, the customer acquisition cost is $120.

CAC = Total Marketing & Sales Expenses / Number of New Customers Acquired

There isn't a universal threshold for CAC across all tech companies, as a 'good' CAC allows your business to attract customers and achieve its long-term growth objectives profitably. CAC and Customer Lifetime Value together help companies assess the cost-effectiveness of their customer acquisition strategies, including marketing and advertising expenses, sales commissions, and software costs for customer acquisition tools.

UX design can significantly impact CAC by optimizing website and app designs with clear calls to action, simplifying and auto-filling forms to reduce time and friction, and utilizing data-driven insights to personalize the user journey by tailoring content and recommendations to individual preferences.

Conducting A/B testing on various design iterations can help to identify the most effective strategies.

Ask Yourself

- How could we design an outstanding product experience that would organically attract, convert, and retain customers so effectively that it significantly reduces our reliance on paid acquisition channels?

CAC Resource

- "Customer acquisition cost formula and tips to improve your CAC." Zendesk. Accessed April 30, 2025. https://www.zendesk.co.uk/blog/customer-acquisition-cost/

Customer Satisfaction (CSAT)

CSAT is a key driver of business success in industries that rely on customer relationships and satisfaction, and gauges customer satisfaction with a product, service, or interaction. It's usually calculated through surveys or polls in which customers are asked a simple question: "On a scale of 1 to 5, how satisfied are you with [product/service]?" There's no universally agreed-upon industry standard for high and low CSAT ratings. However, many organizations use a 5-point Likert scale to measure customer satisfaction.

The context of your business and the specific metrics you're tracking are also factors. A CSAT score of 3 might be acceptable in some industries, while it might be considered a red flag in others. Generally, a high CSAT score of 4 or 5 indicates high customer satisfaction. A score of 1 or 2 is considered low, suggesting low customer satisfaction. Industry standards can vary, so comparing your CSAT scores to industry benchmarks and historical data is beneficial. Industries with this focus include customer service industries, hospitality and tourism, e-commerce platforms, retailers, technology, and software.

My approach to prioritizing Customer Satisfaction (CSAT) through User Experience Design (UXD) centers on dissecting the entire customer journey to pinpoint and resolve areas of friction. Some of the most fulfilling work I've done involved deeply understanding how both customers and customer service agents interact across different support channels. By refining the user experience for both groups, we not only made their lives easier but also achieved tangible business benefits, including a marked improvement in CSAT.

Ask Yourself

- What are the top three drivers of high CSAT scores for our most satisfied users?

- How can we amplify or replicate those 'wow' moments consistently across our product and service touchpoints?

CSAT Resource

- "What is a good CSAT score?" Accessed April 30, 2025. https://www.surveymonkey.com/mp/what-is-good-csat-score/

Gross Margin

Gross margin is the percentage of revenue a company retains after subtracting the direct costs of producing its goods or services. It shows how much money is left from sales to cover operating expenses and generate profit. Gross margin is calculated as:

(Revenue - Cost of Goods Sold) / Revenue * 100

Businesses care about it because it shows how efficiently they manage production costs. According to Warren Buffett, a 40% gross margin is a good rule of thumb and indicates strong profitability. Knowing your gross margin helps a company determine optimal pricing strategies and helps investors feel confident about the health of the business in comparison to its competitors.

UX design can impact gross margin in several ways. The first is reducing or optimizing costs. For example, you might streamline a user experience to reduce the number of steps involved, thus minimizing development time, production time, and expenses. You could create products that last longer, or design for upgradability to lessen the need for full product replacements, thus increasing customer retention and potential revenue through upgrade sales. You might adopt a sustainable design philosophy to minimize adverse environmental impacts while maximizing positive social and economic effects. For example, Google is pursuing net-zero emissions across its operations and value chain by 2030.

Ask Yourself

- What are the most significant touchpoints where our design directly impacts costs, support overhead, customer acquisition, and customer retention?

- How might we optimize these touchpoints to improve gross margin?

Gross Margin Resource

- "How do you calculate gross margin? Use this free online calculator." Xero UK. Accessed April 30, 2025. https://www.xero.com/uk/calculators/margin-calculator/

Net Margin

Net margin is what remains after all the bills are paid. It's the "bottom line" of a company's financial performance. It's an indicator of a company's profitability, used by businesses to make decisions about investments, operations, and future planning. Investors and analysts use net income to assess a company's financial health and to compare its performance with that of other companies. According to Warren Buffett, a suitable threshold for net margin is greater than 20%. The formula for net margin is:

$$\textbf{Net Margin = (Net Income / Revenue) x 100}$$

UX design boosts net income through design-led innovation, enabling your company to explore new markets and command premium prices. Well-crafted marketing materials can also enhance conversion rates and increase overall revenue. You could cut costs by developing products that lower support expenses and reduce customer inquiries. Implementing efficient design practices, such as prototyping and streamlined design systems, can prevent costly development delays and decrease developers' time on UI creation, leading to a leaner, more profitable operation.

Ask Yourself

- How can our design strategy directly contribute to both increasing revenue per user (e.g., through feature adoption, upselling, retention) and decreasing our operational costs (e.g., through reduced support tickets, simplified development, or improved efficiency) to optimize our net margin?

Net Margin Resource

- Grundy, Ryan. "What is net income and why is it important?" Sage Advice UK. January 18, 2024. Accessed April 30, 2025. https://www.sage.com/en-gb/blog/what-is-net-income-why-its-important/

Net Promoter Score (NPS)

Net Promoter Score gauges customer satisfaction and loyalty by asking users to rate how likely they are to recommend the product to a friend or colleague. Customers respond on a scale of 0 to 10. A high NPS of 9 to 10 comes from a 'promoter' user group, who will likely repurchase from you and fuel viral growth through word of mouth.

How likely are you to recommend us to a friend or colleague?

| t at all likely | 1 | 2 | 3 | 4 | 5 | 6 | 7 | 8 | 9 | 10 | Extremely like |

Detractor | Passive | Promoter

Example NPS Score

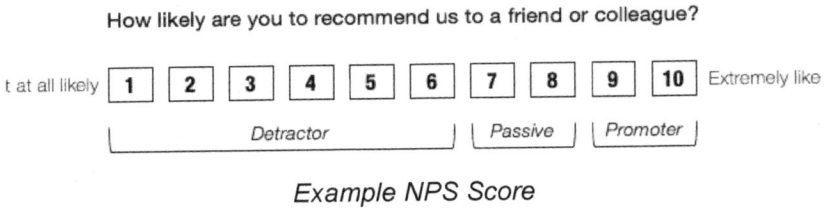

'Passive' users will rate 7-8 and are considered satisfied, but could be more enthusiastic. They are susceptible to competitive offerings and are not included in the NPS calculation.

'Detractor' users will rate 0-6. They are unlikely to recommend the product and are not particularly satisfied with your product or service. Their sentiments could damage your brand and require proactive outreach to mitigate brand damage.

To calculate NPS, you subtract the percentage of detractors from the percentage of promoters. For example, if 60% of respondents are Promoters and 20% are Detractors, the NPS would be 40 (60 – 20). A good Net Promoter Score (NPS) is typically regarded as anything above zero. An NPS ranging from 0 to 30 indicates customer satisfaction, while a score between 30 and 70 suggests strong customer loyalty. A score above 70 is considered excellent, and a score exceeding 80 is classified as world-class, reflecting exceptional customer satisfaction and loyalty.

Regular user research studies can enhance your understanding of how users engage with your product. These insights can help identify areas for improvement. You can achieve this through surveys, interviews, or focus groups to pinpoint pain points and prioritize improvements.

Ask Yourself

- What are the most significant design-related friction points impacting NPS, for Detractors and Passives?

NPS Resource

- "What is a Good Net Promoter Score?" Qualtrics. Accessed April 30, 2025. https://www.qualtrics.com/en-gb/experience-management/customer/good-net-promoter-score/

New User Sign-ups

New User Sign-ups refers to the number of new individuals registering to use a product or service within a specific timeframe. This metric indicates the rate of user acquisition and growth. Tech companies utilize database tracking, event tracking, APIs, and cookies to accurately calculate and analyze new user signups. As a design leader, it's wise to learn how your company tracks this metric, as it directly relates to user experience design.

You can enhance new user signups in numerous ways, for instance, you could allow users to register with either their email or social media accounts, thereby creating minimal friction and delay. You might employ social proof by displaying a notification like, "Over 10 million users buy from us," to reassure potential users that the product or service is popular and reliable. You could add customer testimonials, photos and videos, from satisfied users, or include celebrity endorsements to illustrate the popularity and effectiveness of the product. All these help to build credibility, trust and hopefully more new user sign-ups.

Ask Yourself

- How are we currently measuring the new user signup funnel, and what are the specific points in that journey where users drop off or express confusion, indicating an opportunity for design intervention?

New User Sign-Up Resource

- Olmstead, Levi. "How to Improve & Measure User Activation in 2025 (+Examples)." November 2, 2022. Accessed April 30, 2025. https://whatfix.com/blog/user-activation/

Download this Chapter for Free

How to Download this Chapter to your Inbox

1. **Scan the Barcode:** Open your smartphone camera and point it at the barcode. Your phone will recognize it and show you a web link.

2. **Tap the Weblink:** The link will open a webpage on your smartphone.

3. **Follow Webpage Instructions:** On the webpage, you'll be asked for your email address. This tells your device where to send the free chapter PDF to.

4. **Check your Email Inbox:** The email with the PDF chapter will be from SallyGrisedale.com. If you don't find the free chapter in your inbox, please check your spam or promotions email folders.

We do not share your information with anyone.

CHAPTER 7

Positioning Your Team

DESIGN'S PLACE IN THE TECH BUSINESS ECOSYSTEM

What's the true relationship between your design team and the larger business it serves? And how can you structure your design organization to best support both your team and the company's goals? These are the crucial questions we'll explore in this chapter. We'll gain real-world insights into business strategy and organizational design from Lynn Bacigalupo, who brings a wealth of leadership experience across both UX design and product management.

Throughout your career, you've likely seen design teams play many roles within their organizations. It's vital to understand and align with the business's expectations for these relationships from the outset. If recruiters promise that design is integral to a company's future, only for you to discover it's actually peripheral, you and your team will inevitably face frustration. You'll waste valuable time trying to implement excellent work within a company unwilling or unable to embrace your expertise, because you're attempting to play a role they haven't truly defined or empowered.

When I joined a tech startup, I asked the CEO what relationship he envisioned for design within his company, using the model below as a framework for our discussion. This conversation was incredibly clarifying. We discussed the expectations for design's role in the business, and this alignment allowed me to secure the necessary resources and support to grow the organization.

The relationship between your team and the larger organization it serves can range from being entirely separate to being peripheral, central, or completely integrated. I learned these distinctions from Professor Sabine Junginger,[32] a leading voice in design and Vice Chancellor's Fellow at the University of Northumbria in the UK. This diagram captures each relationship's essence, described in detail below.

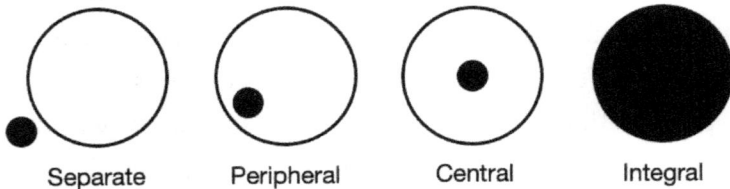

Separate   Peripheral   Central   Integral

---

[32] "PhD Design Sabine Junginger." April 29, 2025. Accessed May 1, 2025. https://www.northumbria.ac.uk/about-us/our-staff/j/sabine-junginger/

Separate Relationship

A separate relationship is where designers, often contractors, are used to address immediate needs, often lacking the strategic oversight of a dedicated design leader. For those employing design resources, the perceived benefit is the agility to iterate quickly and test concepts, potentially bypassing the perceived friction of cross-departmental collaboration and leading to faster progress. Yet, engaging designers in isolation, without the grounding of an integrated design leader and a comprehensive understanding of business realities (technical viability, financial prudence, user desirability), can pave the way for designs that are either technically unachievable or excessively expensive to develop. Also, communication breakdowns and cumbersome handoffs between design and development frequently result in project setbacks and costly rework. Understanding this dynamic—design operating at arm's length—and its inherent opportunities and risks is paramount.

Peripheral Relationship

A design team with a peripheral relationship to the tech business operates at the edges, rather than within the core of the company's strategic and operational flow. It solves specific visual or interaction problems as they arise, but it lacks the deep integration and strategic influence necessary to truly drive user-centered innovation and contribute fully to the company's success. Thus, it is often "doing design for the business" rather than "doing design with the business." It is characterized by limited integration, often reactive engagement. Here's a breakdown of what that might look like.

"Quality is the result of a carefully constructed cultural environment. It has to be the fabric of the organization, not part of the fabric."

Phil Crosby

Reactive Engagement: The design team primarily responds to requests and briefs initiated by other departments (product, engineering, marketing, etc.) rather than proactively shaping the product roadmap or business strategy. They are brought in when a design need arises, rather than being involved from the outset of key initiatives.

Limited Strategic Influence: The team's input on high-level strategic decisions is minimal or non-existent. They are often tasked with executing designs based on requirements defined elsewhere, without a strong voice in determining the "what" or the "why" behind the product or feature.

Siloed Operation: Communication and collaboration with other teams tend to be transactional, focused on specific deliverables, rather than ongoing and deeply integrated. There is often a lack of shared understanding of broader business goals and constraints.

A Focus on Output over Outcome: The team's success is often measured by the timely delivery of design artifacts (mockups, prototypes, etc.) rather than the impact those designs have on key business metrics (user engagement, conversion rates, customer satisfaction).

Potential for Misalignment: Without a deep understanding of the business context, technical limitations, and user needs (beyond the immediate brief), the designs may not fully align with overall business objectives or be technically feasible.

Difficulty Building Deep User Empathy: Due to limited direct interaction and involvement in user research and feedback loops, a peripheral team may struggle to develop a nuanced understanding of the target users and their problems.

Vulnerability and Lack of Investment: In budget cuts or strategic shifts, a peripheral design team might be seen as a less critical function and therefore more susceptible to downsizing or reduced investment.

Limited Career Growth and Impact: Designers working at the periphery may feel less connected to the company's mission and have fewer opportunities to contribute to strategic initiatives, which can potentially impact morale and retention.

Central Relationship

A design team with a central relationship helps businesses identify opportunities, solve complex problems, and create innovative, user-centric solutions that drive business value. They are deeply connected to the 'why' behind the products and services. Here's a breakdown of what that looks like.

Strategic Involvement: Design leaders and team members are involved early in strategic discussions, contributing to product roadmaps, business planning, and even high-level decision-making.

Cross-Functional Collaboration: Designers work closely and continuously with product managers, engineers, marketing teams, and other departments throughout the product lifecycle. This fosters a shared understanding of goals, constraints, and opportunities.

Embedded Within Product Teams: Designers are often embedded directly within specific product teams or business units, fostering a strong sense of ownership and accountability for the user experience of those particular areas.

Shared Goals and Metrics: The design team's success is intrinsically linked to the business's success metrics. They understand and contribute to KPIs for user engagement, conversion, satisfaction, and retention.

Strong Design Leadership Presence: A dedicated and influential design leader (e.g., VP of Design, Chief Design Officer, Head of Design, Design Director) typically sits at a senior level within the organization, advocating for design thinking and ensuring a consistent user-centered approach across the company.

Holistic User Understanding: User research gathers insights and champions the user's perspective across the organization. This deep understanding of the voice of the customer informs both strategic direction and tactical design decisions.

Consistent Design Language and Standards: A team that is central to the business establishes and maintains a cohesive design system and standards, ensuring a consistent and recognizable user experience across all products and touchpoints that works at scale.

Culture of Design Thinking: The design team actively promotes and evangelizes design thinking methodologies and principles throughout the company, empowering non-designers to understand and value the user-centered approach.

Long-Term Vision and Investment: The business views design as a long-term investment and will allocate resources to build and nurture the design function.

Integral Relationship

A design team with an integral relationship to the tech business it serves is deeply interwoven into the company's fabric, functioning as a core strategic partner where design is integrated into all aspects of the organization. Here's a breakdown of its key characteristics.

Strategic Alignment: The design team's goals and initiatives align with the tech company's overarching business objectives and KPIs. They understand the business strategy, contribute to its formulation, and proactively identify opportunities where design can drive value and innovation.

Early and Consistent Involvement: Designers are involved early in the product development lifecycle, participating in strategic discussions, user research, and problem definition alongside product managers, engineers, and business stakeholders. This ensures design considerations are baked in from the outset, rather than being applied as a later layer.

Cross-Functional Collaboration: Seamless collaboration is a hallmark. Designers work closely and continuously with colleagues across different departments, particularly product management and engineering. They participate in joint meetings, share insights and feedback openly, and operate with a shared understanding of constraints and possibilities.

Deep Understanding of the Business: Integrated design teams cultivate a strong understanding of the company's users, market, technology, and business model. They are not just focused on aesthetics but also on the practicalities of implementation, business viability, and user desirability.

Shared Ownership and Accountability: The design team shares a sense of ownership over the product's success and is accountable for its user experience and overall impact. They don't just deliver designs; they actively participate in testing, iteration, and post-launch analysis to ensure their work achieves its intended outcomes.

Embedded Design Leadership: A dedicated design leader often sits strategically within the organization, advocating for design thinking and ensuring the design team's perspective is represented in key decision-making processes. This leader fosters a design-centric culture across the company.

Continuous Learning and Adaptation: The integrated design team actively seeks to understand the evolving needs of the business and its users. They embrace continuous learning, adapt their processes and skills, and proactively contribute to improving the overall product and user experience.

Valued and Respected Function: Design is a critical function that contributes directly to the company's competitive advantage. It is not just a cost center. The design team's expertise and insights are valued and respected across the organization. In tech, an integrated design team is not a separate entity fulfilling requests but an essential partner that deeply understands the business, collaborates seamlessly, and proactively drives value through user-centered design thinking. You are architects of the user experience and strategic contributors to the company's success.

DESIGN TEAM STRUCTURES: PROS AND CONS

With a clear understanding of how your design team's relationship to the business informs your role as a designing leader, it's time to build on that insight.

Next, we'll explore the optimal ways to structure your design function. We'll examine the strengths and weaknesses of different design team models, helping you leverage them to best support the business as an executive leader. This section will cover:

- **Centralized Design Teams:** For driving consistency and strategic alignment.

- **Decentralized Design Teams:** For agility, domain expertise, and embedded impact.

- **Hybrid Design Teams:** For flexibility, integration, and balance.

Centralized Design Team

In large, intricate organizations spanning multiple product lines and business units like Apple, Amazon, Adobe, a centralized design structure often emerges as a powerful model for ensuring high levels of standardization and consistent execution. Here, all designers report to a singular design leader who champions the organization's design standards, guidelines, and product design processes.[33] Overarching corporate and business priorities

---

[33] "What is a Centralized UX Team?" *UserTesting Blog.* Accessed May 1, 2025. https://www.usertesting.com/glossary/c/centralized-ux-team

strategically drive headcount allocation. This allows for dedicated resources to cultivate foundational assets benefiting the company, such as robust UI design systems, shared code libraries, and cohesive brand guidelines. Simultaneously, other designers are embedded within specific product teams or business units, focusing on the design of monetizable offerings.

The strength of a centralized model lies in its ability to cultivate a unified design language and seamless user experience across all touchpoints.[34] This consistency fosters stronger brand recognition, cultivates customer loyalty through familiar interactions, and accelerates project initiation as designers leverage established design systems and processes.

Centralized teams often become fertile ground for designer growth. Close proximity to peers fosters collaboration, knowledge sharing, and mentorship opportunities, uniting designers around common goals that fuel collective creativity and effort. This strong sense of community and shared purpose can significantly enhance job satisfaction and well-being, making centralized teams attractive workplaces.

However, the scale inherent in large tech companies with centralized design functions presents a unique leadership challenge: balancing standardization with individual designer autonomy. While meticulous optimization is critical for maximizing ROI in products reaching millions, leaders must be mindful that designers may feel their impact is less visible. To counteract this, fostering a culture of ownership, actively encouraging innovation through initiatives like design sprints,

---

[34] "Design Team Structure: Ideal Setup for Small, Medium & Large Organizations." *UXPin*. September 24, 2020. Accessed May 1, 2025. https://www.uxpin.com/studio/blog/design-team-structure/

and demonstrating the tangible business impact of seemingly small design contributions are crucial for empowering designers and amplifying the team's overall influence.

Decentralized Design Team

Decentralized design teams flourish in environments where agility and deep domain expertise are essential, often within smaller, swiftly changing organizations or when integrated directly into specific product or business units of a larger company.[35] By placing designers within these focused units, organizations cultivate a deep understanding of the product's unique user base, the nuances of its market, and the overall business objectives. This proximity and daily collaboration with cross-functional partners—encompassing sales, engineering, product management, data science, and marketing—enable designers to create highly tailored and practical solutions that align with the unit's needs.

There is a great example of using a decentralized approach from my time as the design leader for all of Yahoo's media business units' websites. The specific challenge of redesigning the sports website required a level of focused expertise that our centralized designers in UED lacked. Recognizing the ambitious goals set by the General Manager, I knew that a generalist approach wouldn't be enough. I advocated for and ultimately built a dedicated design team with specific expertise in the sports domain. This shift towards dedicated knowledge within the sports business unit highlighted the potential limitations of a fully centralized model when deep specialization is needed for a critical initiative.

---

[35] "What Is A Decentralized UX Team?" *UserTesting*. Accessed May 1, 2025. https://www.usertesting.com/glossary/d/decentralized-ux-team

The resulting success—Yahoo Sports' significant rise in market share—emphasized the importance of aligning design talent directly with specific business goals and the necessity for strategic design leadership to identify and acquire the right expertise, even within a larger organizational context.

Similar to the value that the Yahoo Sports General Manager placed on dedicated design experts, business teams often prefer the responsiveness associated with decentralized product design. This structure enables designers to swiftly respond to market changes and evolving customer needs because they are closely integrated within the problem space. Designers develop deep domain expertise within their business unit, resulting in more nuanced and practical design solutions. This close integration can promote greater autonomy and decision-making power for designers in their product area, potentially speeding up time to market and creating a more agile development process. The extensive product knowledge developed in this model can translate into significantly impactful design outcomes. This visible, measurable contribution—similar to our successful sports redesign focused on user engagement and advertiser appeal—directly benefits the product's success, enhances a designer's portfolio, and strengthens their professional trajectory.

However, the potential downsides of a solely decentralized structure are that designers working within individual business units may face fewer opportunities for broader career development into leadership roles encompassing the entire company and less exposure to cross-functional projects beyond their immediate area. Their impact on the company's overall design strategy and direction may be more constrained, as their primary focus is on the specific needs of their designated product area. This can sometimes limit their ability to engage in strategic design initiatives at the corporate level, potentially resulting in inconsistencies in design language and user experience across various business units if not managed carefully.

Hybrid Design Team

A hybrid design team structure combines centralized and decentralized models. It features a core centralized design team collaborating with smaller, embedded design teams aligned with specific products or business units. This structure is particularly effective for medium-sized organizations managing multiple complex product lines, balancing the need for centralized coordination with the agility of decentralized teams.[36] It enables centralized control over large-scale initiatives, such as global rebranding efforts, while empowering decentralized teams to respond quickly to market changes and focus on specific product features and updates.

However, managing a hybrid structure requires careful planning and coordination to balance the needs of centralized and decentralized teams effectively. A key risk is that decentralized teams may lose sight of the overall design vision, potentially leading to inconsistencies in user experience. Strong design leadership and effective team communication are essential to mitigating this risk. Encouraging cross-functional collaboration facilitates valuable knowledge sharing, allowing designers to learn from one another and stay current on industry trends.

---

[36] Team, Awesomic. "Guide: How To Structure a Winning Design Team in 2024." *Awesomic.* November 1, 2024. Accessed May 1, 2025. https://www.awesomic.com/blog/guide-how-to-structure-your-design-team-in-2024

As a design leader in a hybrid structure, you play a strategic role in shaping the overarching design vision and guiding the organization's design direction. Establishing clear metrics for evaluating organizational skills and the business impact of design work is crucial. This ensures equitable performance evaluation and career growth for all designers, whether part of the central team or aligned with a specific business unit, fostering a fair and empowering environment across the entire design organization.

A hybrid approach can offer the best of both worlds when deciding on the proper organizational structure. It allows for centralized oversight and strategic direction while empowering individual teams to make decisions and respond to specific needs.

Having explored the pros and cons of different organizational structures, it's clear that the optimal model is rarely a one-size-fits-all solution. Each structure's effectiveness hinges on the organization's unique context, size, complexity, strategic priorities, and the desired level of integration.

We've delved into the progression of your design team's relationship with the business, from a separate entity to a fully integrated partner, and examined the strategic choices for structuring your design function. The critical question now becomes: How does this theory translate into practice, especially from the perspective of those who collaborate most closely with design?

To provide a powerful, complementary view, Lynn Bacigalupo offers a compelling dual perspective: not only has she been instrumental in leveraging user experience design teams for Fortune 100 companies, but in her current role as a product manager, she actively champions design's contribution from "across the aisle," delivering impactful solutions that improve passenger experience and optimize transit operations. Her insights will illuminate the practicalities of fostering strong design-product partnerships.

EXECUTIVE INSIGHT WITH LYNN BACIGALUPO

Lynn Bacigalupo is the Global Product Manager for Video Solutions, which includes digital video surveillance and AI analytics, at Icomera in North America. Icomera is the leading provider of integrated connectivity solutions for transportation agencies worldwide. With a strong background in delivering innovative transit technology solutions, Lynn is dedicated to driving customer success and satisfaction. Icomera's onboard digital video solutions support a wide range of use cases that have historically been manual processes, bringing digital efficiency to operational and safety functions. Her expertise in product management, UX design, and cross-functional leadership allows her to consistently deliver solutions that can significantly enhance the passenger experience and optimize transit operations. Icomera's technologies serve millions of passengers yearly and thousands of onboard systems daily.

Before Icomera, Lynn was a User Experience Team Manager at Hathway (now Bounteous), where she led the development of innovative digital experiences for Fortune 100 companies. Before Hathway, she worked as a freelance consultant specializing in UX strategy, research, and business analysis. At MindBody Online, she oversaw U.S. and international marketing initiatives as the digital marketing manager. Earlier in her career, she was a Senior Business

Analyst at MXM (now Accenture) and a UX Strategist at MRM Worldwide (McCann Worldgroup), concentrating on digital strategy, new business development, data analytics, and research.

How did you get into your current position, and what do you enjoy about it?

I started my career in 2003. The first four years were spent in a research strategy role supporting UX. Then, I moved to being a business analyst for five years and used a full spectrum of UX skills for another 8 years working as a consultant and for digital agencies. Agency work is fun; you get exposure to a variety of businesses. However, there was a point where I wanted to focus my career. I joined Icomera with this focus in mind. While I joined to develop my UX skills, I took a project management role to get through the pandemic. I've recently transitioned out of project management to product management. I joke; I only had to change two letters from project management to product management, but the cultural shift has been noticeable.

The global product management team is based at our headquarters in Sweden and operates across the organization. Project execution is within a specific North American region. Our work is quite intricate, and the solutions we manage are complex.

I've had the opportunity to collaborate with a broader range of teams, including a development team in Ukraine. Working with such talented individuals in a war-torn country has significantly impacted my leadership approach. It has reinforced the importance of value-based leadership, recognizing people as individuals beyond their work output. This perspective challenges the callous treatment of employees that is unfortunately prevalent in some organizational cultures. I'm fortunate not to work in such an environment, and this experience has been incredibly rewarding. It's one of the main reasons I've remained with the company and a prime example of how I strive to lead my teams.

Where do UX design and product management overlap, and where do they diverge?

Transitioning from UX to product management has been a significant shift, but I've found that many of my UX skills remain relevant. This week, I'm preparing a presentation for our management team on the progress of my product areas. As I've been working on this, I've realized I'm leaning back into my UX roots.

While the roles might seem different, they share a common goal: designing for the customer. In both UX and product management, the focus is on understanding the user's needs and iteratively improving the product. This involves conducting research, gathering feedback, and ensuring the product meets industry standards and regulations.

Despite the broader scope, I've found that the fundamentals of product design and user-centered thinking remain essential. It's been a refreshing change and a positive extension of my career.

How do mindset and priorities shift from hands-on work to leadership?

My leadership journey began around ten years ago when I realized that leadership can be exercised from any level of the organization. This empowering perspective encouraged me to focus on people and teams, fostering collaboration and connection through shared values.

My role as a leader is to create a space for innovation and problem-solving.

As I progressed in my career, I found that effective leadership involves listening to the organization, understanding its needs, and bridging gaps between different teams. This broader perspective allows me to provide valuable insights and support to individual contributors.

One of my key strengths is my ability to see the big picture and identify opportunities for improvement. By understanding the challenges faced by operational teams and the needs of product teams, I can advocate for solutions that benefit the entire organization. For example, I've challenged the team to rethink our approach to third-party product support, recognizing that a more integrated solution would better serve our end customers.

My role as a leader is to create a space for innovation and problem-solving. By asking the right questions and challenging the status quo, I encourage my team to think creatively and find new ways to deliver value.

What's your typical time horizon for strategic decisions?

When I was working hands-on, my focus was on the immediate deadline. As a project manager, I realized time is a flexible concept. As a leader, my thinking often extends to a five-year timeframe. The future becomes more abstract the further you look ahead, but as you approach it, details become more apparent.

One of my projects involves artificial intelligence in passenger counting (a number that many transit agencies are required to report). While this isn't new, there are many ways to approach it using technology like cameras and sensors. Our solution uses video-based AI.

We must engage with customers to understand their priorities and leverage existing research when considering future AI applications. A recent UIC and McKinsey study interviewed 11 major rail providers globally, identifying areas where AI could improve operations. This helped us narrow our focus on areas that would be truly meaningful for our customers while playing to our organization's strengths. While the most impactful AI application for the rail industry may still be forthcoming, these insights provide a starting point for our future planning.

Several factors drive rail transit, primarily operational efficiency. Delays and disruptions can significantly impact ridership and revenue. While revenue generation is essential, passenger experience is also a key component.

To enhance the passenger experience, transit operators can explore options like at-seat ordering, digital services, tiered internet plans, and safety protocols. However, it can be difficult to tie these features back to increased ridership. Rail transit is often viewed as a utilitarian service, primarily used for commuting or longer trips, but anything we can do to make it more enjoyable is seen as a plus.

How do you consider future market/industry changes in strategic decisions?

One of the most fascinating aspects of working in the rail industry is the stark contrast between its long-term focus and the rapidly evolving world of technology. Railways are built to last for decades, with massive infrastructure projects that can take years to complete. This emphasis on longevity is diametrically opposed to the fast-paced nature of technology.

When considering hardware and AI for railway systems, I have to factor in the relatively short lifespan of computer technology. I need to anticipate the need for upgrades and replacements every few years to ensure the system remains up-to-date. The customer and the technology provider can become outdated if this isn't factored into the initial design.

This friction between long-term infrastructure and short-term technology upgrades is unique to the rail industry due to its highly regulated nature. Customers may be reluctant to update their systems because of the bureaucratic processes involved, even if it means using outdated technology.

How do you use metrics to improve product performance?

Some key performance indicators we use to measure our performance are related to customer interaction, such as the frequency of field visits, conversations, and quarterly business reviews. This lets us listen to our customers and actively understand their evolving needs.

While my goals certainly include product launch timelines, I'm also focused on improving the solution's usability within the company. By collaborating with the operations team, we can ensure that our design solutions cater to the entire organization's needs.

Our solution combines products and services, so it's essential to consider the entire customer journey. The business model is built around this concept, reflected in my performance goals and objectives.

How did your family's history in transportation influence your view of the industry?

The transportation industry has provided a prosperous career for several generations of my family, and I imagine that there are unspoken values that come with that. Maybe the greatest talent is being able to quickly see the interconnections of a system, whether that refers to technology or the overall cooperation it takes to make a service successful.

I recently met up with my father at the annual American Public Transportation Association (APTA) TRANSform conference in Anaheim this year. This was my first time attending, while he's attended for over 30 years. His career in transit started after earning a law degree and working in private practice, which he didn't enjoy as much as he thought he would.

At the conference, he told me many people sort of fell into the transportation industry. They somehow had the opportunity to be in transportation, tried it out, decided they liked it, and stayed there.

There isn't really a standard educational path for transportation, making it also challenging to recruit for this industry. Many people enter the field through unconventional routes. For example, the APTA conference's current chair started her career in hospitality management before transitioning to transportation.

I had never considered a career in transit. I spent many years working for digital agencies, gaining a broad range of experience. However, I sought a role with more focus, complexity, and long-term potential. Working for Icomera has provided me with that opportunity.

My paternal grandfather, who I never met, worked as an aviation mechanic during the war and later for Northwest Airlines. I recently discovered that he specialized in radios and radio frequency technologies, eventually transitioning to flight simulators in the 1960s and 70s.

It's fascinating that he worked with radio frequencies, which are now the foundation of my company's internet services on trains. While not planes, it's still a form of transportation. I feel a solid connection to my family, as this seems like a legacy or a shared family passion.

What are the main obstacles to integrating new tech into public transport?

Any future transport strategy should prioritize improving the passenger experience. This means looking beyond operational improvements and focusing on unique challenges within the rail industry.

For instance, data collection on trains can be costly and time-consuming, especially when real-time data is required. Unlike the tech world, where high-speed connectivity is assumed, rail systems often face limitations regarding connectivity and data costs.

I'm interested in exploring technological solutions that address these industry-specific challenges and significantly impact the passenger experience. By focusing on the rail industry's unique needs, we can identify innovative opportunities for improvement.

For example, we can optimize our systems and reduce expenses by being mindful of data usage and exploring creative solutions. This is just one example of a small problem, but there are likely many more. I don't think this issue is unique to our industry, either. Every industry probably faces its own challenges.

How can AI improve the public transport passenger experience?

I had a colleague who recently joined a company working on autonomous vehicles for the mining industry. It's a niche field, but it's fascinating to see how these future technologies can be applied in such specific and impactful ways. I've also seen how AI revolutionizes agriculture, making farming more efficient and potentially improving food production.

These real-world applications of AI often go unnoticed amid the hype surrounding generative AI and other flashy technologies. As these tools become more integrated into our daily lives, they'll likely become less exciting and more commonplace.

Another interesting aspect of AI is the growing trend of biometrics and technology integration into our bodies. This raises serious ethical questions about the potential drawbacks of excessive technology use and its impact on our mental health. Some people may limit their exposure to technology, while others may embrace it.

Considering how these developments will shape our future and our choices as individuals and as a society is intriguing.

How can PMs ensure effective collaboration with designers and engineers?

I believe it's most effective to approach decisions and discussions within the context of the broadest possible goal to foster cohesion and collaboration among the team. Both engineers and designers are problem-solvers. Presenting the problem to them creates an open dialogue. I invite them to comment on the challenge and ask for their input. This allows them to showcase their thinking and skills and provide valuable insights. By starting with the problem, they're naturally motivated to find a solution.

As a product manager, I've realized that reaching a solution often requires starting where people are. Not all organizations are as advanced in thinking about user experience design as tech giants like Google. Some may be relatively naive, and guiding them toward more sophisticated approaches can be challenging.

It's important to remember that progress, even small steps, is still progress. Organizations vary greatly, and not all will follow the same path. I've learned to let go of certain expectations and be open to different ways of working, particularly decentralized ones.

A Case Study for Improving Network Operations

For example, earlier this year, I identified a need to improve our internal network operations tools. These tools did not adequately support our internal customers, which could ultimately impact our ability to serve external customers.

To address this issue, I engaged with various organizational stakeholders to gather feedback and identify pain points. After compiling this information, I presented it to the relevant teams and asked for their input on potential solutions.

The responses were mixed, with some suggesting that additional information was needed, others expressing concerns about workload, and others prioritizing other projects. Despite initial setbacks, I remained focused on finding solutions and continued to advocate for the importance of improving our internal tools.

I initially approached this project with a traditional consultant mindset, envisioning a structured process of identifying problems, gaps, and costs. However, as I began to engage with teams and delve deeper into the project's complexities, I realized that the traditional approach wasn't going to work. Estimating costs was a significant challenge, as many factors were unknown or uncertain.

I became increasingly concerned about how to move forward without reliable cost information. But as the fall approached, I was pleasantly surprised to discover that progress had been made. The teams I had been working with had taken the initiative to address some of the issues we had identified, and others were now on the roadmap for future solutions.

It was a valuable lesson, highlighting the importance of empowering teams and fostering a collaborative environment. By involving them in the process and trusting their expertise, we achieved results that I hadn't anticipated.

I've come to appreciate that there was a different way of working here. Even by initiating a conversation and asking for help, I inadvertently sparked an unexpected solution. This experience gave me hope and valuable insights into the organization's organic approach.

While this unstructured way of working can sometimes be frustrating, as it may not always feel like you're making progress, it ultimately leads to positive outcomes. The teams involved took the time to consider the problem and identify potential solutions, even if they faced challenges. Their commitment to solving critical organizational problems was evident in their proactive actions.

This experience has taught me to be more open and flexible in my approach to work rather than strictly adhering to a predetermined plan. I don't think the issue lies with me or the organization. If you were to ask other people, I suspect you'd find various opinions on how decisions are made and how organizations move forward.

How do you adapt your approach to product management based on the specific needs of a project or team?

While we use lean startup methods, our long backlog may prevent us from being truly agile. The best approach is a hybrid of methodologies, drawing from waterfall, agile, and lean strengths. Waterfall development can provide focus and alignment, but dependencies must be carefully considered, even in agile environments. Lean innovation is particularly valuable for developing new ideas, but gaps must be filled when scaling these innovations.

Recently, a team member asked why we couldn't launch a technically ready product right away. I explained that launching involves much more than simply releasing the product. Project engineers need to understand how to implement it, the service team must know how to support it, and we require robust monitoring. As we've delved deeper into this process, my team members have developed a better appreciation for the complexities of a successful launch.

CHAPTER 8

Relating to Stakeholders

NAVIGATING THE EXECUTIVE NETWORK

This chapter explores the art and science of forging powerful connections within your professional world. We'll start by mapping the executive landscape and strategizing how to best navigate it. Then, we'll turn inward, examining your internal landscape—your relationship with yourself. Your self-perception and how you communicate internally profoundly shape every external interaction, creating a ripple effect that can either strengthen or undermine your professional rapport.

Next, we'll introduce the four archetypes of relationships: supporters, provocateurs, fence-sitters, and saboteurs. This practical framework will help you decode team dynamics, tailor communication to resonate with individual motivations, resolve conflicts by addressing underlying needs, and build stronger, more effective alliances.

Finally, we'll dive into the critical relationship with design's cross-functional tech partners in product management and engineering. We'll explore key factors for successful collaboration, including invaluable insights from staff engineer Ajay Thakur, who shares his perspective on what he values most in his interactions with design partners.

"The key is getting product partners to value design."
Colin Grigson

The Power of Connection

As an executive, you'll now be regularly interacting with individuals you might have once considered beyond your reach, from the C-suite and senior leadership team to new clients, board members, investors, and legal counsel. This new landscape demands a sophisticated game plan for relationship building that goes far beyond simply reviewing an organizational chart and scheduling introductory one-on-ones, though those are certainly a good starting point.

At the executive level, traditional organizational charts don't fully capture how influence truly flows; organizations function as complex networks of interconnected strategic relationships. Your game plan needs to immerse you in this network, positioning you as a design visionary and thought leader who can genuinely help others excel in their roles. This involves actively seeking to understand their challenges and opportunities through strategic questioning and deep listening. Look for early, low-stakes opportunities for value-add collaboration, and crucially, show genuine interest in them beyond work-related tasks. For more specific strategies on how to achieve this, refer to the "Ask Good Questions and Act on the Feedback" section in Chapter 2. The ultimate goal is to build the rapport and understanding necessary to effectively influence these key stakeholders.

The Price of Disconnect

Without building rapport and ultimately trust within your newly expanded network, you're setting yourself up for challenges. At a minimum, you'll face impaired collaboration and poor communication. At its extreme, the price of disconnect can lead to increased conflict, a hostile work environment, plummeting team morale and productivity, missed opportunities, depleted resources, and a tarnished reputation.

I often made the mistake, in my haste to push projects forward, of failing to step back and truly understand the person across the table from me—to learn what mattered to them, why it was important, and how I might genuinely help. Don't make the same mistake. By intentionally building a robust professional network, you'll unlock your reputation as a trusted leader and a valuable contributor to better business strategy and outcomes.

THE RELATIONSHIP YOU HAVE WITH YOURSELF

Now that you understand why building relationships is essential, let's turn inward and reflect on the nature of your self-perception. As a leader, it's crucial to recognize a fundamental truth: You can only truly control your behavior, not the actions or reactions of others. This understanding forms the foundation of healthy interpersonal dynamics.

Consider this: How do you typically treat yourself? Do you approach your mistakes and shortcomings with harsh judgment, gentle understanding, or detached neutrality? Similarly, how do you view others? Are your interactions colored by critical evaluation, empathetic consideration, or a non-judgmental stance?

"If you judge people, you don't have time to love them."
Mother Teresa

Here's a critical insight: The way you judge yourself and others sends a powerful message, and this message rarely goes unnoticed. Are you currently navigating a critical relationship with yourself, your manager, a direct report, or a crucial cross-functional partner where judgment might hinder progress? It's worth considering whether reframing your internal dialogue and adopting a less judgmental perspective could unlock more positive interactions.

Mother Teresa wisely observed. "If you judge people, you don't have time to love them." This statement highlights that judgment is a barrier to genuine connection and understanding. When leaders are quick to judge themselves, their team members, peers, or stakeholders—evaluating their motives, capabilities, or actions—they immediately erect walls. This prevents the crucial empathetic understanding of individual contexts, challenges, and perspectives that is essential for effective leadership. Instead, a "loving" approach, interpreted as genuine care, respect, and a desire for growth, fosters an environment of psychological safety. In such a space, individuals feel secure enough to share mistakes, offer innovative ideas, and take necessary risks without fear of swift condemnation, unlike the defensiveness spawned by a judgmental leader.

Judgment often fixates on past failures or perceived weaknesses, hindering your own growth and development. A leader who opts for empathy and support focuses on potential, providing constructive feedback and creating opportunities for learning and improvement. This approach builds stronger relationships and trust, as people feel genuinely heard and respected, leading to more open communication and effective collaboration.

By looking beyond surface-level issues, you can dig deeper to understand root causes, leading to more robust problem-solving. This non-judgmental stance also models desired behavior for the entire organization, cultivating a more positive and collaborative culture. Crucially, this principle also applies internally: Leaders who are overly critical of their own past mistakes or perceived shortcomings can inadvertently limit their own potential and self-compassion.

Ultimately, Mother Teresa's wisdom reminds leaders that effective leadership is not about constant evaluation, but about deep engagement. It's about leading with compassion, striving to understand before being understood, and prioritizing the growth and well-being of both their people and themselves. This non-judgmental approach to self and others unlocks greater potential, builds more resilient teams, and ensures more sustainable success.

THE FOUR ARCHETYPAL RELATIONSHIPS

What does your landscape of professional relationships look like? Drawing inspiration from the foundational work of Carl Jung, we can observe four fundamental archetypal relationship patterns that offer a robust framework for navigating workplace interactions strategically. For our discussion, we'll label these key dynamics as:

1. **Supporters**: Your champions and allies.

2. **Fence-sitters**: Those who are currently neutral or undecided.

3. **Provocateurs**: Individuals who challenge your ideas and assumptions.

4. **Saboteurs**: Those who actively undermine your efforts.

Supporters

A supporter actively champions your growth, well-being, and success. This manifests in various ways, including advocacy, where they stand up for you, recommend you for opportunities, and ensure your contributions are recognized.

Have you ever worked for a supportive leader? What was it like to have them delegate effectively to you, believe in your decisions, and offer autonomy? Did they shield you from unnecessary stress, office politics, and unfair criticism while ensuring you have the resources and support necessary to thrive? Did they consistently show recognition and appreciation by acknowledging your achievements, celebrating your successes, and expressing their gratitude? Does working for them make you feel good, motivated, engaged, and productive? Does working with them give you a sense of belonging and a feeling of value and respect?

That's the archetype you want to be and have! When you find a supporter, thank them and ask what you can do for them because supporters perform large and small acts of thoughtfulness every day for others without thinking. For example, I remember being in a project review meeting where PMs and engineers were discussing a name to put on a button in the user interface. The conversation was heated, and suggestions were getting out of the realm of good UX design best practice. I suggested we schedule a follow-up meeting once the content strategist could be part of the meeting and share their research findings and recommendations for how best to label the button.

Fence-Sitters

Fence-sitters are indecisive and hesitant to commit to a course of action. They evade a definitive stance on issues and prefer to remain neutral or undecided, even when a decision is required. They might connect with elements of various viewpoints but hesitate to support any of them entirely. This fence-sitting behavior often arises from a fear of making the wrong choice and facing negative consequences or criticism, which is understandable. Such behavior can be heightened by a desire to avoid conflict, challenges in weighing risks and rewards, a quest for perfection that leads to over-analysis, and a lack of confidence in their decision-making abilities. We've all experienced situations where the stakes are high and emotionally charged, and the thought of committing to speak or act can feel like a daunting and losing proposition.

You can learn to recognize this behavior in people who avoid taking a stance on a new strategy, remain neutral during team conflicts, or hesitate to commit to a project until they see how things unfold. It might be a manager who delays making critical decisions, shirks responsibility for challenging situations, or fails to provide clear direction to their team. You may also notice it in customers who express interest in a product but hesitate to buy, continually comparing options without reaching a definitive decision. Alternatively, it might be a cross-functional partner who shows interest in collaboration yet hesitates to commit while keeping other possibilities open. In tech, we refer to this as CYA: Cover Your Ass behavior. We've all engaged in it and seen it happen. However, in leadership roles, indecisiveness can create confusion and ambiguity among team members, hindering clarity regarding expectations and priorities.

When unsure about what to do, sitting on the fence and expending energy worrying, the better course of action is to clear the confusion by taking action. The cost of not committing is missing opportunities, allowing others to capitalize on the situation at your expense. Ongoing uncertainty and a lack of direction will undermine you and your team's morale. Indecisiveness can erode trust within the team, as members might question your leadership ability to make sound judgments.

Recognizing fence-sitting behavior, whether in yourself or others, is pivotal for leadership. Instead of prolonged contemplation, the key lies in proactive engagement. Fence-sitters are not necessarily resistant; often, they lack sufficient information, clarity, or confidence to take a definitive stance.

Your role as a leader is to engage these individuals actively. Creating space for their concerns and questions can make them feel genuinely heard and understood. Ensure they grasp your proposals, the underlying rationale, and the desired outcomes. People naturally gravitate toward collaboration when they feel secure in your leadership and clearly understand mutually agreed-upon goals.

Building trust and rapport with fence-sitters requires dedicated effort and consistent follow-through. By patiently nurturing these relationships, you empower yourself and the fence-sitters to collaboratively identify solutions and potential courses of action that you can confidently support together. This inclusive approach encourages individuals to move off the fence and enhances the decision-making process with diverse perspectives, ultimately strengthening both your team and your initiatives.

Provocateurs

A provocateur intentionally sparks discussions or controversies, often by presenting unconventional views or challenging the status quo. They may question established practices, promote debate and critical thinking, and advocate for innovation and change. Provocateurs excel at prompting a team to think creatively and explore new approaches. The benefit of having a provocateur is that they stimulate debate and discussion, which can prevent complacency and drive critical thinking, leading to more robust decision-making and a deeper understanding of issues.

Provocative behavior can stem from various sources. Personality traits like intrinsic curiosity, nonconformity, and a desire to challenge norms often drive individuals to question assumptions and standards. It could be driven by a cognitive style of analytical thinking, critical reasoning, or a passion for debate that leads people to provoke. Provocateurs often identify blind spots in existing strategies, helping you or the team avoid costly mistakes and improve performance. They may also continuously push for improvement and anticipate potential challenges and disruptions, allowing for the development of contingency plans and effective adaptation to change. When channeled effectively, a provocateur can be a valuable asset for any organization.

It's not always easy to be around someone who naturally seeks flaws in arguments and challenges conventional wisdom, especially if it's driven by a need for attention or a desire for power rather than a genuine wish to improve a situation.[37] When their actions become disruptive, be bold and address them directly and professionally as a leader. If a private conversation isn't feasible, address them respectfully in public. Everyone deserves clear boundaries for respectful communication and debate, so encouraging the expression of views constructively is essential. Building rapport with a provocateur may require time and patience. This can be challenging, but staying calm and using respectful language to avoid provoking emotional reactions is essential.[38] Redirecting the conversation back to the task can help minimize disruption and reinforce the significance of achieving larger goals, for example, "To ensure our meeting is productive, please limit side conversations and stay focused on the agenda." Scheduling a private follow-up allows for a more constructive

---

[37] Ruddle, Nick. "Managing Disruptive Employees: Restoring Harmony and Productivity in the Workplace." ActionCOACH. June 21, 2023. Accessed May 4, 2025. https://westessex.actioncoach.co.uk/2023/06/21/disruptive-employees/

[38] "Building rapport in the workplace." SEEK. May 20, 2024. Accessed May 4, 2025. https://www.seek.com.au/career-advice/article/building-rapport-in-the-workplace

discussion. This approach prioritizes maintaining a professional working relationship over personal friendship and protects your reputation by managing complex interactions with composure and focus.

Saboteurs

A saboteur undermines. If the saboteur is a colleague, they may sabotage your work to boost their reputation, secure a promotion, or earn a bonus. This could involve taking credit for your ideas, withholding vital information, or spreading negative rumors about your performance. They might resent your success or perceived advantages, prompting them to derail your efforts out of spite. Personality conflicts or differing work styles can lead to sabotage, even if unintentionally. The consequences can hinder your career by impeding advancement, damaging your reputation and mental health, and potentially leading to job loss. Saboteurs create a toxic work atmosphere, which might include poor morale, widespread trust issues, and a decline in overall productivity by teams or individuals.

Confronting saboteur behavior is incredibly stressful and challenging. To prevent distractions from the saboteur, focus on your work and strive to deliver high-quality results while maintaining a positive attitude. Document each occurrence, noting the dates, times, and actions taken, and seek support from trusted colleagues.

The common saying regarding those you spend time with is, "You are the average of the five people you spend the most time with," often attributed to motivational speaker Jim Rohn. The individuals you surround yourself with influence your thoughts, habits, behaviors, and ultimately, who you become. Select your colleagues and collaborators thoughtfully, and surround yourself with people who inspire, support your goals, and uplift your spirit. This isn't just about pleasantries; it's about safeguarding your energy, fostering innovation, and ensuring your efforts are recognized and valued. When you're amidst a team that challenges you positively, celebrates your successes, and offers genuine assistance during hurdles, you thrive. Their support acts as a catalyst, propelling you further toward your aspirations and making the journey more fulfilling.

If you are unable to find this at work, consider leaving if you can, so you can find a role in a company that is supportive and aligned with your values. Your professional well-being is paramount. Staying in an environment that drains you, stifles your growth, or doesn't appreciate your contributions is a disservice to yourself and the hard work you've invested. Seek out workplaces where your "pearls" are not only recognized for their value but are also part of a larger, respectful exchange that benefits everyone.

DESIGN'S CORE PARTNERSHIPS: PRODUCT MANAGEMENT AND ENGINEERING

As design leaders, two partnerships are absolutely crucial for your success: engineering and product management. These roles are deeply intertwined, operating in close collaboration on a daily basis during daily stand-ups, sprint planning, and backlog grooming sessions, collectively addressing questions and contributing to critical decisions involving technical feasibility, customer desirability, and business viability. While daily work overlaps significantly, each discipline holds a unique, high-level responsibility during product development:

- Design establishes the **what**, defining the user experience and the solution's form.

- Engineering explains the **how**, determining the technical implementation and bringing the design to life.

- Product management clarifies the **why**, articulating the problem, market need, and business value behind the product.

To succeed, all functions must understand each other's areas, priorities, and limitations and remain open to giving and receiving constructive feedback. Valuing each other's expertise and a willingness to compromise fosters a genuine partnership. I've mentioned this is the ideal, so what is the reality?

> *"People fail to get along because they fear each other;*
> *they fear each other because they don't know each*
> *other; they don't know each other because they have not*
> *communicated with each other."*
> *Martin Luther King, Jr.*

Conflict in tech between cross-functional teams is common. The best thing you can do to support your team is to have an open dialogue with your PM and engineering counterpart. Strengthening this partnership will increase the chances of creating better products. The best way to achieve this is to understand the roles everyone plays, the responsibilities they carry, and the critical metrics they are accountable for. For example, product managers are accountable for the product's success in the marketplace. Their responsibilities include defining the product vision, strategy, and roadmap in alignment with the company's business objectives. Their KPI's fall into these main categories:

- **Business impact:** These metrics measure the product's overall contribution to the business and might include average revenue per unit, monthly and annual recurring revenue, and customer lifetime value.

- **Product performance:** These metrics assess the product's functionality and efficiency and might include acquiring new customers, conversion rates, traffic volume, and daily active users. These metrics help determine whether the audience is growing or shrinking.

- **User-centric metrics:** These evaluate how users engage with the product and might include the time it takes to complete tasks, the number of errors during a task, the number of active users, the bounce rate, and customer satisfaction.

Design and product management share interdependent responsibilities. The PM's roadmap directly impacts your design strategy. Design research and user feedback drive product decisions and design execution to realize the product vision, making collaboration essential for alignment between product strategy and design execution.

A strategic partnership with product management hinges on a shared understanding of business goals and a commitment to measurable outcomes. By proactively identifying and aligning on KPIs, you can demonstrate your direct impact on business success, fostering a collaborative relationship built on mutual accountability and shared objectives.[39]

The same is true when collaborating with engineers who are accountable for building and implementing technology, ensuring it is reliable, high-performing, efficient, and secure. When you understand their goals, constraints, and priorities for implementing your designs, you cultivate trust and develop mutual respect.

Key Performance Indicators (KPIs) for engineers in tech are typically categorized to provide a holistic view of performance.

- **Delivery and throughput** measure how efficiently and quickly a team can release working software, focusing on the speed and flow of development.

- **Quality and reliability** KPIs hone in on the stability, robustness, and maintainability of the software, ensuring what's delivered is sound.

- **Efficiency and process** metrics examine the health of the development pipeline, highlighting areas for internal improvement.

- **Impact and business value**, which are a shared responsibility with design and product management, also significantly contribute to KPIs related to demonstrating how their work drives business goals.

---

[39] "Chief Product Officer: Role, Responsibilities, Salary & More." Accessed May 4, 2025. https://productschool.com/blog/career-development/chief-product-officer

- **Team and developer experience/health** metrics focus on the well-being and overall effectiveness of the engineers themselves, recognizing that a healthy team is a productive one.

An excellent way to deepen your engineering knowledge is to have a casual meeting where you can safely ask questions like this:

- What significant technical challenges do you anticipate if we pursue this design idea?

- What, if any, potential workarounds or trade-offs should we consider?

- What are our technology or infrastructure's current 'hard limits' that significantly impact user experience?

- How likely are those limits to change in the next six months or one year?

In my conversation with Uber's staff engineer and head of cognitive computing, Ajay Thakur, graciously answered all my engineering questions. As a result, I gained firsthand insight into the technical constraints of data availability, API limitations, and network bandwidth that Uber faces. For clarity, I briefly explained the key engineering terms used in our interview at the end of the chapter, in case this information is new to you, as it was for me.

EXECUTIVE INSIGHT WITH AJAY THAKUR

Ajay Thakur is a name synonymous with innovation at the forefront of technology. With over two decades of experience, Ajay has spearheaded the development of cutting-edge products across various domains. At Uber, Ajay leads the Center of Excellence for Generative AI, spearheading its first production deployments and achieving significant cost savings. He also played a crucial role in developing a scalable architecture for deploying chatbots across various channels. This platform has resulted in substantial cost reductions and growth opportunities for Uber. Before joining Uber, Ajay held leadership positions at companies like 247.ai, where he directed the development of omnichannel conversational bots for enterprise clients. He also has a strong background in big data analytics, implementing solutions for major organizations such as AT&T and Microsoft.

Ajay's background combines technical expertise with business acumen. His impressive educational credentials, including an MBA from a joint program between the Haas School of Business and Columbia Business School, strengthen his solid engineering foundation. This unique blend enables him to navigate the technical complexities and strategic elements that drive successful technological innovations. In my interview with Ajay, I explored his remarkable journey and insights into the ever-evolving world of technology, where we unpack his experiences and gain valuable perspectives from this engineering pioneer.

What do you like best about being an engineer in the tech industry?

I've always been drawn to the idea that my work can make a tangible difference in people's lives. From my early days at Cisco, where I helped develop technologies like Power over Ethernet functionality, which allows you to power your device with your ethernet cable, to my role at Uber, where I focus on improving the experience for earners and customers, I've had the privilege of seeing firsthand how technology can shape the way we communicate and live.

It's rewarding to know that my efforts empower first-generation earners in many countries, create opportunities for single mothers and immigrants, and ultimately positively affect countless individuals.

The challenge of problem-solving keeps me coming back for more. There's a unique thrill in tackling complex technical issues and finding innovative solutions. I appreciate the tech industry's empathetic and culture-shaping nature. Compared to other fields, tech has the power to challenge biases and promote inclusivity, which is something I value deeply.

What defines a genuinely impactful engineering product?

From an engineering perspective, massive success is about developing solutions at scale that have a profound and lasting impact on society—creating an invisible legacy that extends far beyond the product or service—where people can rely on technology to empower them, bridge divides, and solve pressing global challenges.

Given the emphasis on speed, flexibility, and continuous improvement, why do you favor Agile methodologies for product management?

I prefer an Agile manifesto for speed, hyper-communication, and the flexibility to deliver a minimal-regret product. Agile is a project management approach that breaks the project into phases and emphasizes continuous collaboration and improvement. The emphasis on collaboration, communication, and delivering value in small increments aligns perfectly with my goal of creating impactful products.

How do you balance the need for innovation with stability and maintainability?

When balancing innovation with stability and maintainability, I prioritize the end goal. By ruthlessly prioritizing features, I've found that "less is more" often leads to better outcomes. I lean on proven frameworks and components to achieve scalability and build a solid foundation. It's crucial to start with the right choices, like selecting appropriate messaging systems, databases, and protocols.

Adopting a cloud-first approach helps us reduce costs down the line. I leverage journey data to gather effective feedback and iterate on product designs. Whether it's readily available or needs to be implemented by our developers, this data provides invaluable insights.

How do you measure an engineering team's effectiveness?

I prioritize tangible deliverables that directly contribute to the product's success. This means focusing on writing code rather than excessive documentation and delivering solutions rather than simply counting lines of code.

Additionally, I believe in the importance of leadership within engineering teams. Engineers can significantly contribute to positive outcomes by helping others grow, contributing to the company's overall goals, and reducing friction within the team.

Ultimately, these metrics are closely tied to the broader product goals and objectives. Market share is a crucial indicator of success, and it's achieved by delivering products that create magical customer experiences.

Velocity, defined as the speed at which we deliver value, is crucial for maintaining competitiveness. Ensuring customer satisfaction and providing functional and enjoyable products are also vital. By reducing bugs and fostering a positive user experience, we can cultivate loyal customer bases and achieve lasting success.

How can AI be leveraged to revolutionize product development?

I'm excited about artificial intelligence's potential to revolutionize product and user experience design in the coming decades. AI can transform our work, making us exponentially more efficient and effective. Imagine leveraging AI to scale our engineering capabilities, turning a single engineer into a team of hundreds. This would allow us to tackle complex problems faster and create more sophisticated and innovative products.

Additionally, AI-powered user interfaces could dramatically simplify the user experience by making predictions and anticipating our needs. For example, an AI-powered shopping app could recommend products to users based on their past purchases and browsing history. This would lead to more intuitive and enjoyable interactions with technology, making it accessible to a broader range of people. Engineers will need a strong foundation in AI to stay competitive and meaningfully contribute to the future of product design.

What are effective strategies for communication between designers and engineers?

Design is the crucial link between our technical creations and the end-users who interact with them. While engineers pour their hearts and souls into building functional and efficient products, designers shape the user experience.

I believe in fostering deep partnerships with designers to ensure our engineering efforts align with user needs. By understanding their vision and goals, we can work together to overcome challenges and deliver products that delight our customers. Open communication is vital; sharing technical constraints and discussing potential limitations helps designers make informed decisions that are both feasible and impactful.

I've encountered challenges in collaborating with design teams, but I've found that the most successful partnerships occur when designers have a solid understanding of technical constraints. A good designer knows what is achievable within our engineering limitations and can push back constructively to ensure we strive for maximum utility in our products.

What are the critical factors for collaboration between designers and engineers?

Effective collaboration between design and engineering hinges on open communication and shared understanding throughout product development. Starting early in the scrum planning phase allows both teams to align on goals and expectations. By being involved in the testing phase, designers can ensure that the final product meets the original design intent.

Clear communication of design concepts, such as interaction flow-charts, is crucial for bridging the gap between the two teams. Providing context for design choices, backed by journey data and customer feedback, helps engineers understand the rationale behind the proposed solutions. Documenting final decisions, whether through a JIRA ticket or a visual representation, ensures everyone is on the same page. (JIRA is a software platform for project management and issue tracking.)

From a technical standpoint, designers need to be mindful of constraints such as data availability and API limitations, as these can impact the feasibility of specific design elements. Striking a balance between design simplicity and engineering complexity is also critical, as overly complex designs can delay development. Network bandwidth and data costs must be considered for real-time products to ensure a seamless user experience.

"Open communication is vital; sharing technical constraints and discussing potential limitations

helps designers make informed decisions that are both feasible and impactful."

How can you ensure our designs are right before you build them?

It is essential to make it easy for customers to report bugs or provide feedback. Dogfooding our products and utilizing dashboards helps us identify areas for improvement and iterate quickly. Dogfooding involves testing a newly developed product or service by a company's staff before making it available to customers.

What factors can affect a project's timeline and quality? How can you minimize the risks?

As an engineer, I have encountered several key risks affecting product development timelines and quality. One of the most persistent challenges is the need for a clear vision. Without a well-defined understanding of what we aim to deliver for our users, it becomes challenging to prioritize features and allocate resources effectively.

Another obstacle is the tendency toward analysis paralysis, where excessive decision-making can lead to delays and inefficiencies. Determining whose opinion is most important, the VP's or the customer's, can be a delicate balancing act.

The advent of generative AI has introduced a new layer of uncertainty. While this technology offers immense potential, its outputs can be unpredictable, making establishing robust quality control measures essential.

How can AI enhance design-development synergy?

I'm incredibly excited about the future of product design and development. With the aid of AI, we can reduce wasted user effort by automating repetitive tasks and providing personalized recommendations. Additionally, the shift toward data-driven decision-making will enable us to make more informed choices based on real-world evidence rather than relying solely on intuition. Predictive analytics will become increasingly prevalent, allowing us to anticipate user needs and proactively address potential issues.

ENGINEERING TERMS USED BY AJAY

Data Availability

Ajay highlights that Uber's real-time location data dependency necessitates robust data availability. To mitigate slow, unreliable, or inaccessible data, engineers must implement advanced error handling, caching, and backup strategies, which increase code complexity and development time. Furthermore, inconsistent data complicates system management, requiring engineers to differentiate between data outages and code bugs, hindering effective system monitoring. This unreliability can render real-time features, like dashboards and personalized recommendations, impractical.[40]

---

[40] "Overview | Maps JavaScript API | Google for Developers." Accessed May 4, 2025. https://developers.google.com/maps/documentation/javascript/overview

API Limitations

An API, acting as a software interface like a car's controls, allows programs to communicate. However, restrictions on its functionality can hinder feature development, as specific endpoints or data may be inaccessible, preventing a personalized experience. Performance suffers from rate limits, causing slow or unresponsive applications. Scalability and reliability are also affected; APIs unable to handle high request volumes can fail as user bases expand, impacting apps like Uber. Development becomes complex, requiring workarounds like caching, which complicate maintenance. Cost considerations arise from usage-based APIs, demanding careful resource allocation. Finally, security risks emerge if limitations are poorly managed, potentially enabling denial-of-service attacks, and requiring engineers to prioritize protective measures.[41]

Network Bandwidth

This is the amount of data transferred, and its cost is a technical constraint. Higher bandwidth means more data but also higher costs. Complex designs need careful justification based on business and user needs, using research and data, especially when exceeding engineering limits or requiring extra effort from engineers.[42]

[41] "API Management - Amazon API Gateway - AWS." Accessed May 4, 2025. https://aws.amazon.com/api-gateway/

[42] "Bandwidth (computing)." Wikipedia. February 5, 2008. Accessed May 4, 2025. https://en.wikipedia.org/wiki/Bandwidth_(computing)

Key Factors for Successful Design & Engineering Collaboration

Ajay highlighted several critical factors that underpin effective collaboration between design and engineering teams. He emphasized that seamless partnership thrives on proactive communication and a shared understanding of the product development lifecycle. He underscored the value of early involvement for designers in the Scrum planning process. This allows for mutual alignment on objectives, early identification of potential technical constraints, and a more holistic approach to problem-solving from the outset. He noted the importance of designers participating in the testing phase, ensuring the final implementation accurately reflects the intended user experience and design vision.

Clear and contextual communication of design concepts emerged as a cornerstone of successful collaboration. Ajay pointed out the effectiveness of interaction flowcharts in conveying design intent. He also stressed the significance of designers providing the 'why' behind their design decisions, grounding their proposals in user journey data and valuable customer feedback. This context helps engineers understand the user-centric rationale driving the design choices. Finally, Ajay highlighted the need for meticulous documentation of final decisions, whether through platforms like JIRA or visual aids, to maintain clarity and alignment across both teams.

From a technical perspective, Ajay offered valuable insights into the constraints designers should consider. Data availability and API limitations can significantly influence design feasibility, and early awareness of these can prevent rework and frustration. He also emphasized balancing design ambition and engineering complexity, recognizing that overly intricate designs can introduce development delays. For real-time products, Ajay noted the critical need to consider network bandwidth and data costs to ensure a smooth and efficient user experience.

By embracing these principles of open communication, early engagement, contextual design rationale, clear documentation, and an awareness of technical constraints, design and engineering teams can forge stronger partner-ships, leading to more innovative products and services.

CHAPTER 9

Lighting the Way for Future Leaders

After three decades of immersing myself in the dynamic world of technology as a UX designer and a leader, my focus has shifted to empowering the next generation of creative leaders. Coaching and guiding aspiring individuals like you is my most incredible privilege and, I believe, my most important work.

Although exhilarating, the journey into executive leadership is seldom without its complexities. The demands can be relentless, the challenges multifaceted, and the need for a strong support system is critical. The email below, from a coachee who recently took on the role of VP of Design, vividly illustrates the intricate realities of executive leadership in tech:

Hi Sally!

How've you been?

I'm so sorry for not replying all this time. It has been crazy busy here, and I am settling in well.

Last week, I was part of a large group attending the Sales Kick-off for the new financial year. The company has set its target annual recurring revenue for the year ahead.

My design team is good. I find a lot of relief in having a team that focuses on the actual design work, while I am part of various discussions around vision, planning, and estimation.

The company culture here is putting out fires, one after another, and never having time to breathe. The "fires" here are customer asks, as well as requests for various proof-of-concepts from the sales folks (which are always treated like actual feature development work but expected to be done in a ridiculous timeline of 3-6 weeks).

My big project is the complete UX overhaul of the product. This is a massive exercise, but again, we are expected to deliver it while being fully available for all other firefighting tasks. I am exploring various options (mainly AI tools) for executing this. I have reached out to a friend to help me out with it. So far, I have had no success in that field.

I met the 30-day onboarding plan, but I completely missed setting up the 60-day plan after that. I believe

I am handling the role well, but it is still early. I want to reevaluate it in a few months.

The founders are difficult personalities to work with and are too closely involved with various aspects of the product. I wish it were different, but we all work with what we've got.

P.S. As I wrote this email, I got pulled into a call where the co-founder asked me to email the CEO about my current work status and updates. He was upset about something design-related yesterday, and I was working remotely, and he kinda started believing that I am not "present." So today will be spent drafting that email for him.

As you can see from this candid account, the transition to a senior leadership position brings a tidal wave of responsibilities: navigating ambitious growth targets, leading a team while simultaneously contributing to strategic discussions, contending with a culture of constant urgency, spearheading massive projects under tight deadlines, and even managing the expectations and working styles of founders. The need to quickly adapt, prioritize effectively, and maintain presence and impact, even while working remotely, becomes paramount.

This email underscores several key takeaways that we've explored throughout this book: the importance of a strong and focused team, the necessity of clear communication and expectation management, the value of strategic planning (even amidst chaos), and the inevitable interpersonal dynamics that come with leadership. It also subtly highlights the need for external support and guidance during significant career transitions.

Surrounding yourself with the correct levels of support, whether it's a trusted mentor, a supportive peer network, or an experienced coach, is not a luxury but a necessity for navigating the complexities of executive leadership. Having someone to offer perspective, share strategies, and provide a sounding board can be invaluable in maintaining focus, preventing burnout, and ultimately, thriving in your role.

I hope the insights, interviews, and strategies this book shares will serve as a valuable guide as you embark on your leadership journey. The path ahead will undoubtedly present its own unique set of challenges. Still, by cultivating strong relationships, understanding team dynamics, mastering self-awareness, and seeking support, you will be well-equipped to navigate these complexities and inspire and empower the teams you lead. The future of creative leadership in tech rests on your shoulders, and it is my sincere honor to play a part in helping you illuminate that path.

Sally Grisedale

Sally Grisedale is a leading expert in product design who has built and led user experience design teams worldwide for major tech firms like Yahoo, Apple, and Meta. Since 2019, she has run her coaching consultancy focused on helping future creative leaders reach and sustain top executive roles. She holds an MA from the Royal College of Art and is a Fellow of the Royal Society of Arts (FRSA). She also graduated from the Co-Active Training Institute's CPCC program and Harvard Business School's AIGA Business Perspectives for Design Leaders Executive Program.

She authored *"Leading by Design"* after realizing from her own experience that there is a lack of support and guidance for creative leaders at the highest levels of industry as executives. When she's not coaching, she enjoys gardening at her home in the Lake District of England. You can view her coaching work at https://www.sallygrisedale.com and subscribe to her newsletter https://www.leadingbydesign.coach.